MW01610712

nine
ideas
you
should
know

before i go

god loves you
the bible is alive
heaven starts now
the kiss of justice and mercy
the tricycle of faith
god is _____
god's game plan for you
jesus' third way
your identity is in christ

paul loewen

before i go
Copyright 2017 Paul Loewen
All Rights Reserved
ISBN-13: 978-1543055733

Edited by Carl Degurse
Cover design by Paul Loewen

For full-res images, keynote presentations,
questions, comments, or to contact Paul email
pauldloewen@gmail.com.

table of contents

to the douglas youth

introduction

Over the past 10 years, I have led around 500 youth events, 25 retreats, and 20 multi-day service trips. It has been a phenomenal experience, and I get sad when I think of leaving - I will miss you all! I leave not because I'm tired, bored, or done with this kind of work in any way. I leave simply because there is more to learn, more to do, and more ways to grow.

This year, I have done a "best-of" my devos taken from the past 10 years. Some are repeats, some are combinations of one or two (or five) devos, and some are new to this year. Basically, as I organized the schedule and thought through what I would teach, everything had to pass through a filter asking, "If they don't know this, am I okay with it?" If the answer was yes, I passed the topic over. These nine devos represent ideas I believe are foundational to a lifelong, vibrant, inquisitive, and world-changing faith. In particular, they aim to help in transitioning from the black-and-white world of the early years to the grey areas you encounter in adulthood. These nine ideas are not all I could say; I probably could have come up with ten more. But we only had limited time, and there is something to be said for being concise.

At the same time, I am aware knowledge will only take you so far. These chapters are either aimed at the **head** or **heart** (information or emotion). Since it's much easier to convey information than emotion in a book format (as opposed to the conversational setting where we originally had the devos), these chapters try their best but may easily miss the mark on emotions. The third part of the triad is **hands** (action). That's thoroughly impossible to convey in a book, so I didn't even try (other than, from time to time, the practical applications of what we were learning).

When it comes to both heart and hands, I ask you to look back at the experiences of the last year (or more): giving piggyback rides at Zion Kids Club, bowling with seniors at Bethania, being exhausted on day eight of SOAR, staying up late on retreats, laughing together at our hilarity, lamenting together at the world's brokenness, worshipping our God together around a campfire, and more. For those reading this who didn't participate in the youth program this year (or any other), keep in mind what's contained here only conveys a portion of what we have gone through together.

For the youth who are now young adults, for those not a part of youth with me around, it is up to you to discover the emotional aspect of faith in community and the active part in service to your brothers and sisters in your neighbourhood and around the world.

This book is mostly the **head** part of the triad, and it's largely up to you to fill in the **heart** and **hands**.

To the youth I say this: I am sad to leave, but excited about the future in front of you. There are so many big and amazing possibilities in store as you seek God. Faith may not always make the most sense (though I hope these nine chapters help), but I can promise you following God is never boring.

With that in mind, may I remind you of nine ideas you should know **before I go**...

before
i go
1
god loves you

"The Lord merely spoke, and the heavens were created. He breathed the word, and all the stars were born." That's Psalm 33:6, and you probably already forgot it. It's good stuff, but it's nothing mindblowing. Let's see if we can change that.

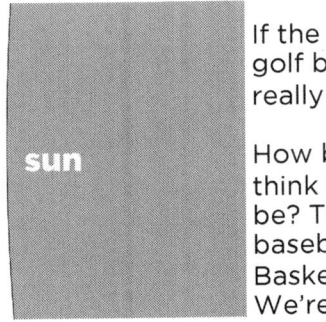

If the earth were a golf ball, you'd be really small.[1]

How big do you think the sun would be? The size of a baseball? Softball? Basketball, maybe? We're thinking way too small - it would be about fifteen feet across, big enough to stretch across the youth-room risers,

---

[1] Much of this section takes its inspiration from Louie Giglio's "Indescribable."

with the top exploding its way into the foyer upstairs and the bottom ripping a hole in the floor.

Since it's so big, it's a terrible idea to have the tiny earth so close to a flaming ball of fire. If the earth were a golf ball, the sun would be as far away as Donwood Manor, halfway to John Pritchard.

You could fit a million of those golf-ball earths inside of that sun.[2]

Let's go bigger.

Meet our next star: Betelgeuse.[3] Betelgeuse is a beast.

earth (too small to show)
○ **sun**

betelgeuse

It's twice as big as…

If you said, "The sun," you're wrong. It's twice as big as the earth's orbit around the sun. If the sun is at Donwood Manor, that means the earth on its orbit would pass from church, over the houses in the neighbourhood, and swing through John Pritchard on the other side. Take that distance, and double it. Now you've got the size of Betelgeuse.

If you put golf-ball earth on the surface of Betelgeuse,[4] the other side of Betelgeuse would be on top of the Chief Peguis Bridge, over the Red River.

Let's go bigger.

---

[2] Almost as many as I've lost when playing golf.

[3] Pronounced "Beetle Juice."

[4] A very bad idea.

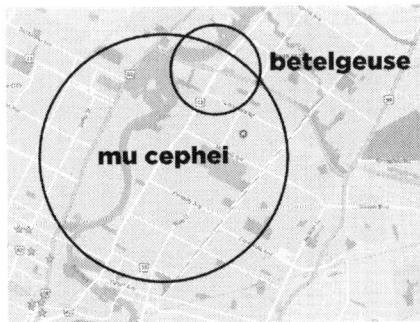

Mu Cephei is one of the largest and brightest stars in our galaxy. If the earth were a golf ball, Mu Cephei would stretch from Douglas all the way to the Redwood Bridge, the bridge going from Henderson into the North End. If you were to replace our sun with Mu Cephei, it would swallow up all planets up to Jupiter.

Let's read that verse again, "The Lord merely spoke, and the heavens were created. He breathed the word, and all the stars were born." (Psalm 33:6)

It has more significance now, doesn't it? Feels a little grander, heavier?

A long time ago, I received a "100 Verses to Memorize" book. I opened it and did the first one. I memorized it well, but I never got past it. In some ways, I didn't have to. It's 1 John 3:1, and it says, "See what great love the Father has lavished on us, that we should be called children of God! And that is what we are!"

In many ways, it's all I needed to remember. Believe it or not, that same God that **breathed** (note: metaphor) the stars into existence has called each and every one of us, of you, a child of God. That's only a little insane.

We went from small (ourselves) to big (the stars) back to small (ourselves) and now we land ourselves in this weird paradox: small in size but big in meaning. And it points to the beauty and the mystery of something as grand as love. Something you can't put on a scale and you can't scientifically measure (at least, not that I know of). And yet something as massive and incredible and terrifying as a God who can breathe stars can love something as small and insignificant and trivial as me or you.

Mind. Blown.

If you hadn't been singing "Jesus Loves Me" all your life, and you hadn't grown up in the church, and you had experienced nothing but hatred or dislike from people in your life, the idea that God loves you would knock you to your knees. It's that big; it's that significant.

Sometimes we have a hard time understanding what the word **love** actually means, since we throw it around when we talk about pizza. Let's start by focusing on what love is **not**:

Love is not distant.
God is not off in His massive living room somewhere, with his experimental Earth going off the rails while He dozes.

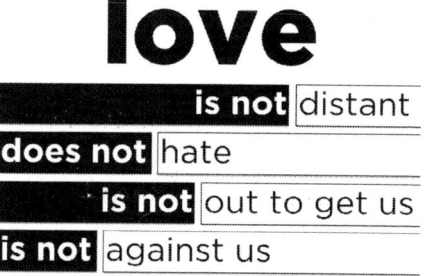

Love doesn't hate.
Sounds simple, right? I mean, we shouldn't even have to say it. But it's true, some people think God hates them. Maybe they've done terrible things, maybe they assume they're hated by everyone. Either way, God doesn't hate. Love doesn't hate.

Love isn't out to get us. It's not hard to picture a world where things are out to get us. After all, Murphy's Law (a real thing, look it up) says what can go wrong will go wrong. Murphy's Law is what makes it seem like every lane in traffic is slower the instant we get in it, like everything we have sucks in comparison to everything else, and why no one likes us. It would be possible to think it's God slowing the traffic down or spilling the yogurt on our last pair of pants, but God's not out to get us. That's not what love does.

Love is not against us. Again, should be self-explanatory. In the song "You Make Me Brave," (Bethel Music) a lyric always stands out to me. The singer says, "For You are for us, You are not against us." The fact this is in the song means they think it needs to be clarified. Which means someone, somewhere, thinks God is against them. Love isn't against us.

I've spent the whole time so far talking about the fact God loves us and loves you. This is option 2 of a 1-2 option:
1. God doesn't love us
2. God loves us

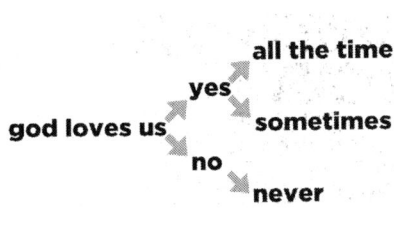

I hope I've convinced you (in your head) it's option number 2. But still, there is wiggle room for more interpretation. You see, we could say God loves us, yes, but it's only **sometimes**. As in, when we're good, or studying our Bibles, or listening to Christian music at the expense of a good beat. Here's the thing, if I were to put out a poll like this...

When does God love us?
1. All the time
2. Sometimes

9

paul loewen

...there are plenty of people who would know they were supposed to answer **all the time,** but in their heart they only act like He loves them **sometimes.** That's a problem. Here's why:

In Romans 5:8, Paul says, "Jesus loved us while we were still sinners." That's right, there's no confession or conversion or absolution or commitment needed to earn God's love. In fact, the word earn is a terrible word in the above sentence. We don't **earn** God's love. We can earn favour and future blessings, but God's love is the only offer from God that is not based on conditions. As in, there is no fine print.

It is only God's love that is offered to everyone universally, no matter what religion, race, gender, orientation, occupation, past, present, or future. If I am willing to accept God loved me when I was still a sinner (and still am), I have to be willing to accept God loves others the same way. This applies to the friend who gossips, the businessperson who cheats their partner, the terrorist that killed innocents, or any personal enemy we may have in our lives.

It's just the way it is, and denying God exists or living your life to prove Christians wrong won't change that. It can change a lot, but not the fact God loves you. It's His only unconditional promise.

I will introduce you to a video of Brennan Manning, the author of a book called "The Ragamuffin Gospel." He has been the inspiration for songs, books, and even a Christian band. His words have touched people all over the world. Below is the text of what he says in the video, but you'd be best off jumping on Youtube[5] and seeing/hearing it for yourself.

---

[5] https://www.youtube.com/watch?v=pQi_IDV2bgM

In the 48 years since I was first ambushed by Jesus, in a little chapel, in the mountains of Western Pennsylvania, and in literally the thousands of hours of prayer and meditation and silence and solitude over those years, I am now utterly convinced that on Judgment Day the Lord Jesus is going to ask each of us one question, and only one question: "Did you believe that I loved you? That I desired you? That I waited for you day after day? That I longed to hear the sound of your voice?"

Brennan Manning
National Speaker and Author

The real believers there will answer, "Yes, Jesus, I believed in your love and I tried to shape my life as a response to it."

But many of us, who are so faithful in our ministry, in our practice, in our church-going, are going to have to reply, "Well, frankly, no sir. I mean I never really believed it. I mean I heard a lot of wonderful sermons about it, in fact I gave quite a few myself. But I always knew that was just a way of speaking, a kindly lie, some Christian's pious pat on the back to cheer me up."

And there's the difference between the real believers and the nominal Christians who are found in our churches across the land. No one can measure like a believer the depth and intensity of God's love. But at the same time, no one can measure like a believer the effectiveness of our gloom, pessimism, low

self-esteem, self-hatred, and despair that
block God's way to us.

Do you see why it is so important to lay hold
of this basic truth of our faith? Because you're
only going to be as big as your own concept
of God. Remember the famous line of the
French philosopher Blaise Pascal? "God made
man in his own image, and man returned the
compliment?" We often make God in our own
image, and He winds up to be as fussy, rude,
narrow-minded, legalistic, judgmental,
unforgiving, unloving, as we are.

In the past couple of years I have preached the
gospel to the financial community in Wall
Street, a thousand physicians in Nairobi, I've
been in churches in Chicago, St. Louis, Miami,
Seattle, and, honest, the God of so many
Christians I meet is a God who is too small for
me, because He is not the God of the Word,
He is not the God revealed by and in Jesus
Christ, who this moment comes right to your
seat and says, "I have a word for you: I know
your whole life story, I know every skeleton in
your closet, I know every moment of sin,
shame, dishonesty, and degraded love that
has darkened your past. Right now I know
your shallow faith, your feeble prayer life, your
inconsistent discipleship, and my word is this: I
dare you to trust that I love you just as you
are, and not as you should be, because you're
never going to be as you should be."

Sometimes our God is too small. We think
something we've done, said, or thought can
possibly interfere with the way God loves us. It
can't. God's love is unconditional, it's the single
biggest idea God wants you to think about when
you think about Him. Not His justice, His wisdom,
His power. His love. It stretches from the very

furthest corners of the world into the smallest and darkest corner of your heart, the corner you haven't shown to anyone and never will.

He loved you before you were born, before you came to know Him, before you did anything for Him. No matter your past, present, or future, the love of God is reaching out to you. Don't ever forget that.

Someone took the time to pull the verses that speak about how God thinks about us into one place, and to rewrite them to be from God's perspective, putting them all into a letter. Just like with the Brennan Manning text, I put it here but you'd benefit from watching the video[6] and having it read to you.

My Child,[7]

You may not know me,
but I know everything about you.

Psalm 139:1

I know when you sit down and when you rise up.

Psalm 139:2

I am familiar with all your ways.

Psalm 139:3

Even the very hairs on your head are numbered.

Matthew 10:29-31

For you were made in my image.

Genesis 1:27

In me you live and move and have your being.

Acts 17:28

For you are my offspring.

Acts 17:28

---

[6] https://www.youtube.com/watch?v=6TcxA_7_fi8

[7] Father's Love Letter used by permission
Father Heart Communications ©1999
FathersLoveLetter.com

paul loewen

I knew you even before you were conceived.

Jeremiah 1:4-5

I chose you when I planned creation.

Ephesians 1:11-12

You were not a mistake,
for all your days are written in my book.

Psalm 139:15-16

I determined the exact time of your birth
and where you would live.

Acts 17:26

You are fearfully and wonderfully made.

Psalm 139:14

I knit you together in your mother's womb.

Psalm 139:13

And brought you forth on the day you were
born.

Psalm 71:6

I have been misrepresented
by those who don't know me.

John 8:41-44

I am not distant and angry,
but am the complete expression of love.

1 John 4:16

And it is my desire to lavish my love on you.

1 John 3:1

Simply because you are my child
and I am your Father.

1 John 3:1

I offer you more than your earthly father ever
could.

Matthew 7:11

For I am the perfect father.

Matthew 5:48

Every good gift that you receive comes from
my hand.

James 1:17

For I am your provider and I meet all your
needs.

Matthew 6:31-33

My plan for your future has always been filled
with hope.

Jeremiah 29:11

Because I love you with an everlasting love.

Jeremiah 31:3

My thoughts toward you are countless
as the sand on the seashore.

Psalm 139:17-18

And I rejoice over you with singing.

Zephaniah 3:17

I will never stop doing good to you.

Jeremiah 32:40

For you are my treasured possession.

Exodus 19:5

I desire to establish you
with all my heart and all my soul.

Jeremiah 32:41

And I want to show you great and marvelous
things.

Jeremiah 33:3

If you seek me with all your heart,
you will find me.

Deuteronomy 4:29

Delight in me and I will give you
the desires of your heart.

Psalm 37:4

For it is I who gave you those desires.

Philippians 2:13

I am able to do more for you
than you could possibly imagine.

Ephesians 3:20

For I am your greatest encourager.

2 Thessalonians 2:16-17

I am also the Father who comforts you
in all your troubles.

2 Corinthians 1:3-4

When you are brokenhearted,
I am close to you.

Psalm 34:18

As a shepherd carries a lamb,
I have carried you close to my heart.

Isaiah 40:11

One day I will wipe away
every tear from your eyes.

Revelation 21:3-4

And I'll take away all the pain
you have suffered on this earth.

Revelation 21:3-4

15

I am your Father, and I love you
even as I love my son, Jesus.
John 17:23

For in Jesus, my love for you is revealed.
John 17:26

He is the exact representation of my being.
Hebrews 1:3

He came to demonstrate that I am for you,
not against you.
Romans 8:31

And to tell you that I am not counting your
sins.
2 Corinthians 5:18-19

Jesus died so that you and I could be
reconciled.
2 Corinthians 5:18-19

His death was the ultimate expression
of my love for you.
1 John 4:10

I gave up everything I loved
that I might gain your love.
Romans 8:31-32

If you receive the gift of my son Jesus,
you receive me.
1 John 2:23

And nothing will ever separate you
from my love again.
Romans 8:38-39

Come home and I'll throw the biggest party
heaven has ever seen.
Luke 15:7

I have always been Father,
and will always be Father.
Ephesians 3:14-15

My question is...
Will you be my child?
John 1:12-13

I am waiting for you.
Luke 15:11-32

Love, Your Dad
Almighty God

If the words you just read didn't sink in, read it again. Read it over and over until you can anticipate the next verse just as you finish the last one. These verses are God's truth, poured out into your heart and soul in a way that can change the way you think and the way you act. And it all starts when you let it hit you in your heart, because once we recognize God's love and claim it as truth in our lives, we have the confidence and the backbone to go out and be the kind of people God calls us to be.

That's it. All this for three words:

God.
Loves.
You.

before
i go
2 the bible is alive

Love it or hate it, the Bible is something we deal with a lot. And there are **so** many things we could say about the Bible. In all reality, everything this book contains will come from there, so I think we could agree we better figure out what we think of the Bible. There are a lot of fundamental questions we can ask when it comes to the Bible:

1. Where do we get the Bible?
2. Why do we trust the Bible?
3. How should we think about the Bible?
4. How should we use the Bible?
5. Is there a story running through the whole Bible?
6. What is the story of the Bible?

At first I thought I would tackle all six questions in thirty minutes. Then I realized that, given my tendency to talk and talk and talk and talk...we'd be there for 8 hours and I probably still wouldn't be done. And then I realized I've addressed five out of the six topics in my time here at Douglas, most of them within the last two years.[1]

So let's focus on the question, "How should we think about the Bible?" And here's why: first, because it's the one I haven't addressed before. Second, because it's the one lying behind the other five. If we get this one right, the other ones should make more sense (in other words, if we think about the Bible right, we're more likely to use it right, etc.). Third, it's a harder topic to talk about than the other ones, and the one that's open to the most debate. Fourth, it has the biggest implications for how you hold your faith in the years to come, particularly as you face challenges to what you believe.

Let's dig in!

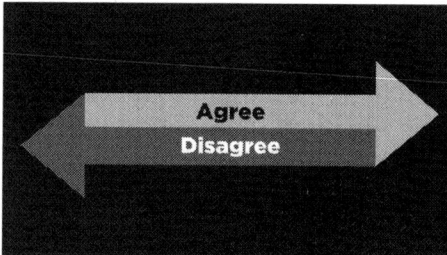

I will make statements, and you decide whether you agree. In the youth room, we label one wall "Agree" and the other "Disagree;" you can go all the way to the walls or stop at any point on the line. If you're in a room by yourself, put the right wall as "Agree" and the left wall as "Disagree." Get up and move yourself with each upcoming statement. (If you're somewhere public and don't want to move to walls, take anything from your pocket and put it in front of you - to move it to the right is "Agree" and to the left is "Disagree.")

---

[1] I addressed #1 every time we do a Bible presentation for the Junior Youth, #2 in February of 2016, #4 in April of 2016, and #5 and #6 in both Faith Exploration classes as well as the Riverton trips. Junior Youth, I know you haven't experienced either of those last two, but I didn't want to repeat them for the Senior Youth.

For each one, move **before** you read the rest of the thoughts on the topic. So stop after the bolded part and move, then continue once you're standing in your place on the spectrum.

The Bible is the Word of God. Where did you place yourself? Why are you there? Answer it out loud if no one's around. There's a lot of interpretation that comes with this statement. What is meant by **Word of God**? Does it mean God spoke it out loud? Not necessarily, since Jesus himself is also called the Word. In that case, does it mean the clearest explanation of who God is? Hebrews 4:12 says, "For the word of God is alive and powerful. It is sharper than the sharpest two-edged sword, cutting between soul and spirit, between joint and marrow. It exposes our innermost thoughts and desires." I'm not going to interpret "Word of God" for you now, but get ready for the next one.

The Bible is boring. Where did you place yourself? Why are you there? Answer it out loud if no one's around. Depending on which part you read, you could say a nice and loud **YES!** or a **NO!** The Bible is an incredibly diverse book. It's got all kinds of craziness: epic sagas of kings and nations, love stories that would rival Hollywood, one of the most counter-cultural movements ever to hit the planet, and letters from friend to friend we're allowed to snoop on. So if you opened it to a random spot and think it's boring, most people would agree with you. That's okay. Boring isn't always bad - we can still learn from it. But don't miss out on the exciting parts.[2]

---

[2] The book of Joshua is an intense war story. The book of Ruth is a great love story. The Psalms are the place to go if you're emotional and need to vent or cry. The book of Daniel is just a good story, period. Matthew, Mark, Luke, John, are all great little novels that tell the story of Jesus. Start in any of those places until you feel comfortable to venture out beyond them.

paul loewen

The Bible is a story. Where did you place yourself? Why are you there? Answer it out loud if no one's around. It's not a story in the traditional sense, because it was not written by one author and doesn't contain only one perspective. It's fascinating; some people are averse to calling it a story because that might make God a character within the story (as opposed to the author). You see, a story is usually about someone who wants something, and goes out to get it.[3] If that's the case, and the Bible is a story, we've got God as the main character. What does God want? The Garden of Eden forever? Well, that didn't happen. Eternal happiness for everyone? Yes? No? Everyone's not happy right now, but will we be? The other challenge of seeing the Bible as a story (with God as the main character wanting something), is they don't like thinking God, with all His power, might not get what He wants. If you haven't thought of the Bible as a story, try it. It gets kind of interesting. What's the plot? Climax? Resolution? Foreword? Epilogue?

The Bible inspires me. Where did you place yourself? Why are you there? Answer it out loud if no one's around. I purposely worded it this way. I could have said, "The Bible is inspiring." That's more about someone **else** than it is about our own experience, and this time I want your experience. There are definitely parts of the Bible that aren't inspiring (genealogies, anyone?), but there are other parts that are mind-blowingly amazing. Take, for example, Ruth's commitment to her mother-in-law in Ruth 1, "Don't ask me to leave you and turn back. Wherever you go, I will go; wherever you live, I will live. Your people will be my people, and your God will be my God. Wherever you die, I will die, and there I will be buried." That's quite the

---

[3] A great book about this is Donald Miller's "A Million Miles in a Thousand Years."

commitment. Or maybe take a look at the Psalms if you're looking for inspiration. They're a great place to start.

The Bible was written by God. Where did you place yourself? Why are you there? Answer it out loud if no one's around. Here's the thing, this is different than the first one ("The Bible is the Word of God"), because we can consider it the word of God without agreeing God wrote it. The way you see this one has a lot to do with how you were raised. If you feel like you're betraying someone (a parent or pastor, maybe) by putting yourself over by "Disagree" on this one, take a deep breath and let it go. There's no point in lying to yourself. The Bible may be inspired, sacred, and even holy, but we have a good idea it was written by people. And the beauty of that? If we remember who wrote it and when it was written, we can get closer to what it originally meant. Anyone, even those who say it was written by God, should want that when they come to the text.

The Bible has no mistakes. Where did you place yourself? Why are you there? Answer it out loud if no one's around. I'm not talking here about grammar, though the idea of us judging the grammar of a different language written several thousand years ago is ludicrous. You might not know where to place yourself if you're not sure what I mean by **mistakes**. Let's look at the reverse: if the Bible didn't have mistakes, it would always agree with itself. It would always make sense. It would even make sense on a line-by-line basis, and wouldn't contradict anything we experience in reality (for instance, if the Bible says the sky is purple and it's not, we've got a problem). This question is starting to get at the word **infallible**, which I'll talk more about later. You might not have known where to put yourself on this one, and I understand.

paul loewen

The Bible needs interpretation. Where did you place yourself? Why are you there? Answer it out loud if no one's around. Interpretation is hard, because it's where we start to differ as Christians, and where disagreements arise. I'm sure some of you have thought, from time to time, "Why can't it just be simpler?" That's not a bad question, but then it wouldn't be as fun :). What's crazy about the Bible is the layers of interpretation it requires, and the layers of understanding that went into it. First, there is the fact that it happened during a time of different cultures. Just the way we wouldn't expect a three-year-old to understand, "It's raining cats and dogs" or "Hold your shorts," we can't expect to understand what was going on two thousand years ago (and what their equivalent phrases were). Similarly, they'd be baffled if they tried to understand a modern texting conversation full of emojis. Second, the writers had certain ideas and intentions when they were putting it together. For instance, Matthew is telling the story of Jesus to Jews, people who knew the Old Testament. Luke is telling it to a Greek-speaking disciple who had no knowledge of what went on. Mark is just being snappy and telling it quickly, probably showing us being on the outside is not a bad thing, and often the insiders get it wrong. John is totally different, doing the most interpretation of events himself.[4] Then we've got to take it and somehow reinterpret it into today's world. It's not an easy task. And you thought being a pastor was all games, snacks, and goofing off.

---

[4] An interesting example of this: John 3:16, the most famous verse in the Bible, comes in the middle of a long paragraph. In the Greek, there is no punctuation like, "This," that shows someone is talking. So at the beginning of the paragraph Jesus is talking (we can figure that out from the context), but by the end we're pretty sure it's the narrator talking. So, where did the transition from Jesus' words to an explanation of Jesus' words happen? Who said John 3:16? Was it Jesus or John?

The Bible can always be understood. Where did you place yourself? Why are you there? Answer it out loud if no one's around. This one goes hand-in-hand with the above one. If it needs to be interpreted, then we're opening ourselves up to different interpretations. If there are different interpretations, some will be easier and some will be harder. And some might not make sense. While I think the Bible can always **mean** something to someone, there are giant leaps we have to make as interpreters that are challenging. We can't easily understand the culture of the story, or even the intentions of the author. If we could sit them down and interview them, that would be great!

The Bible is a vital part of being a Christian. Where did you place yourself? Why are you there? Answer it out loud if no one's around. For about 1900 years, the Bible has been the way it is. For the first 70-100 years of the church, there was no Bible as we know it today. Believe it or not, Christians and the church have been around longer than the New Testament. That doesn't mean it's not **vital**, it's just not the **only** essential in our faith. Community, tradition, Holy Spirit - these all played significant roles in the early church and they still should today. Without spoiling too much of what I'm going to get to, the Bible is one of the best ways we can connect to God: it's a story of people reaching up, God reaching down, and all the messiness and confusion that brings.

The Bible matters today. Where did you place yourself? Why are you there? Answer it out loud if no one's around. In some ways, it feels like the world is moving past the Bible, away from looking at one view as God's truth for the world. It's sad that sometimes it's the people who love the Bible the most who damage its effectiveness in society by holding it to a standard for which it was never meant. My hope is this chapter can give you a healthier and more accurate perspective on the

Bible so, in a hundred years, your great-great-grandchildren still find it relevant the way it was meant to be.

We're done. You can sit and stop looking like a weirdo pacing back and forth. I hope that exercise was helpful for you - sometimes forcing yourself to plant yourself on a spectrum can clarify your beliefs. First, recognizing that rarely are you in a fully YES or fully NO position is helpful. Second, it's good to move.

Let's go back to what I just said, because an irrefutable-book-that-you-can't-argue-with is probably the best explanation for how people like to use the Bible. It's not exactly the definition of the word **infallible**, but it's usually what people mean when they use that word. Infallible is not a word in the Bible, though the Bible does speak about itself (more on that in a bit). Infallible is rather an idea we've projected back onto it, based on the fact that the circumstances around the writing, assembling, and translation of the Bible have been guided by God's Holy Spirit.

There are dangers that come with treating the Bible that way. Let's look at each of them.

Danger 1: If it's challenged you have to chuck it out. If the Bible is its own witness, and if you're not allowed to argue with it, and if it's always the textbook you use to answer every question with 100% backing, you're going to one day get challenged in a way you can't fight. When that happens (by a friend, family member, teacher, etc.), you will need to admit the way you've held

onto the Bible doesn't stand up to reality. Though it's not your only option for reacting, some people chuck out the entire Bible at that point.[5]

Danger 2: It becomes stale and boring. If the Bible speaks for itself, if every statement only has one interpretation, then soon you will tire of it. Your perspective is stuck, you're unwilling to change, and you're not open to the Bible speaking to you in new and exciting ways.

Danger 3: It can be used as a weapon. This one hurts, and it sucks. Honestly, it's frustrating to see people use the Bible this way. This is what people are doing when they say, "The Bible says you're a sinner." They use it to shut down conversation, shut out other people or religions, or push their own agenda.

Danger 4: It's irrelevant in society. Here's the deal: we're not living in a world where everyone believes in the Bible. When we were,[6] you could use it as the basis for your arguments, your governments, and your authority structures. But if I walk up to a random person on the street and say, "The Bible says you should do this," they can easily just say, "I don't believe in the Bible, so that doesn't matter to me." And, to be honest, it's true. Why should they agree with something they don't believe in and don't hold to be truthful?

Danger 5: Other religions can do the same thing. There's nothing stopping me from claiming the Harry Potter series as my sacred Scripture, and saying I'm going to live my entire life according to lessons learned in it. It's the same way other

---

[5] One other common reaction would be to deny evidence that is directly in front of your face.

[6] More accurately, that might say, "When we thought we were."

religions can take any book they'd like and hold it up and use it as a weapon or tool. If we can treat our special book that way, so can they. And they can claim any book that says anything.

If that is how **not** to see the Bible, you might wonder how we **should** see it. We'll start off by asking what the Bible says about itself. There's an inherent problem in this: it's strange to explain a book by saying what it says about itself. Here's a brain-tease for you: "This sentence is wrong." Try to figure out if that sentence is telling the truth. You can't, because it's internally got a problem. Same way we can't use what the Bible says about itself as full-on evidence for what the Bible is. Again, any book could claim to be anything it wants to. So, even if the Bible decided to say it is the infallible word of God written by God Himself, we couldn't trust that. It's just not evidence enough (hint, it doesn't make those claims about itself). Here are a few insights it shares:

"Fix these words of mine in your hearts and minds; tie them as symbols on your hands and bind them on your foreheads. Teach them to your children, talking about them when you sit at home and when you walk along the road, when you lie down and when you get up." That's from Deuteronomy 11:18-19, and it talks about the **usefulness** of the Bible in teaching, reminding, helping, guiding, and leading. Fantastic stuff.

"All Scripture is God-breathed and is useful for teaching, rebuking, correcting, and training in righteousness, so that the person of God may be thoroughly equipped for every good work." That's from 2 Timothy 3:16-17, and is probably the most used of the four verses I'll show you. The phrase "God-breathed" is the tough one, and is usually translated as "given by inspiration of God." The challenge: it only shows up once in the Bible, which makes it significantly harder to figure out what it means. Here's the deal: God-breathed (or inspired, or however you want to phrase it) doesn't mean **infallible**. It could, if it was used that way elsewhere or if the Bible was described as infallible somewhere else.

"These things are written so that you may believe that Jesus is the Christ, the Son of God, and that by believing you may have life in his name." That's from John 20:31, and he's referring specifically to the last 20 chapters of the book he's written. The point here is simple: the purpose of **this** book is to convince you that Jesus is who he said he is, and to get you to the good stuff: life!

"So that you may know the certainty of the things you have been taught." That's from Luke 1:4, and he's talking about the book he's starting: Luke. Luke is concerned about evidence, about making sure you got the times and dates all correct and that it's clearly documented. That's why he's talking like this.

Here's the deal: the Bible says a lot about itself (although when it does, it's usually talking about other parts, like in 2 Timothy he's talking about the Old Testament), but it doesn't say there aren't errors. What's remarkable is the Bible has been well-researched and proven to be remarkably accurate historically, and it's been tested time and again in people's lives to be accurate when it comes to describing human nature, relationships, and hope. It's got an incredible track record.[7] When something in life completely echoes what I find in the Bible, I find myself frequently thinking, "Maybe Jesus knew what he was talking about..."

---

[7] This was part of what I talked about in the Bible study on "Why do we trust the Bible?"

paul loewen

So I'm going to get honest here. What I want to say isn't believed by every Christian, and some would consider it controversial and un-Christian.

But the fact is the Bible existed **after** the church, meaning there was a church without a Bible. Part of the design of the Bible is the tension we feel when we read it; there are stories of people wrestling with God (metaphorically and literally), and this beautiful book we ended up with is the result of those struggles. By holding it too high, and claiming it's something it's not, we're at risk of damaging it, misusing it, and making it irrelevant in a society that doesn't recognize it as an authority any more.

Rather, we need to look at it as a fresh and alive document telling of God's desire to get to know people, and people's efforts to get to know God. Along the way it speaks from different perspectives in different ways, so it might not always agree with itself. Understood in this way, the Bible can withstand whatever anyone can throw at it; it can survive the time of your life when black and white becomes grey, when many young Christians abandon the old perspective because they don't know a Christian can hold other perspectives. It's versatile, flexible, and alive. It's able to inspire, correct, lead, challenge, and downright befuddle those reading it.

The craziest part is, if you let it, it might even change you.

before
i go

heaven starts now

Ever since I can remember, I wanted to skydive. So, the summer I turned 18, a friend and I booked tandem jumps in Gimli to divebomb out of an airplane. When you skydive (for the first time), there are two options: solo or tandem.

If you choose to go solo, you need about five hours of instruction/teaching, the plane goes only a few thousand feet up, and your chute opens immediately after you jump. At that point you float and aim for the target, hoping your landing is as soft as a marshmallow.

To get as much free fall as possible, you go tandem. There's less instruction, but you're strapped to the front of an instructor's harness. The plane goes up much higher (in my case, to about 9,000 feet), and you plummet for about thirty seconds together.

I chose tandem. So I'm strapped to my instructor's chest, tucked in the back of a rickety airplane, squished beside my friend and his instructor (who looks like Doc from "Back to the Future"), and we putter down the runway and take to the skies. As the plane climbs, my instructor and I try to converse (at scream volume, mostly sounding like this, "WHAT DID YOU SAY?"). Finally, we're at the right altitude.

He pops the door open, and a 100-mph wind rushes into the cabin. Without really warning me (and, if he had tried, I probably wouldn't have heard) he leans over and looks outside. This is all fine, except I'm strapped to his chest. Where he leans, I lean. Our faces hang out the side of an airplane 9,000 feet in the air, and he's looking at the ground to see if we're almost at the right spot.

He seems satisfied, so we turn towards the door. He grabs both sides, and yells at me to put my feet on a small step underneath the plane's wing. I do what he says, and now I'm sitting on about three inches of plane, with my legs out the door, holding nothing. He yells something along the lines of, "I'm going to push us out on three, and we'll tuck into a flip."

Then we're tumbling forward. He wasn't joking about the flip - airplane, sky, ground, airplane, sky, ground. At some point I see another mass of bodies emerge from the airplane and I know my friend is following me down.

Skydiving is kind of like floating,[1] and it's an incredible sensation.

---

[1] I've also been bungee jumping. That's a different feeling. When you jump, it only takes a few seconds to get from the platform to the bottom of the bounce, so the ground is rushing up at you like nobody's business. Skydiving, though, is so high up that you don't feel like you're falling (I never got the stomach-in-the-throat feeling), instead you feel like you're floating on top of a 120-mph wind that's determined to make your mouth look ridiculous as it flaps around.

We fall for our predetermined thirty seconds, keeping an eye on the altimeter strapped to my chest. When we get to about 4,500 feet, I pull the chute and experience a bit of whiplash as we slow to a float, thanks to the giant, billowing canvas above our heads. He shows me how to steer and we swing left, right, then go into a few spins. By pulling on both sides at the same time we can make the parachute wing collapse, which means we drop again before the chute catches air and stops us.

As we're floating nicely, we look around. To the side I see my friend. We're far enough away that we won't collide, but close enough that I can wave and attempt a yell. We're almost at the level of the clouds, and my instructor points out a rainbow. What's cool about being up in the air is that rainbows always put you in the middle, but normally the pesky ground gets in the way of seeing the whole thing. So, up in the air, we can see it's a full rain-circle. We aim towards it, and our shadow appears on the cloud in front of us.

"Can we fly into the cloud?" I ask.

He is silent for a minute, but then, quietly, agrees. We head towards it, the rain-circle getting smaller and smaller as we approach the water droplets creating it, and plunge into the cloud.

It's completely **disappointing**.

First, it's wet. Second, you can't see very far. Third, it's not a fluffy marshmallow like I'd hoped. We turn around, pop out the bottom of the cloud, and I wipe my face.

Below is our target: a circle of gravel about one hundred feet in diameter. He tells me to lift my feet when he says to, and he'll absorb the impact. We're probably about five hundred feet from the ground

33

paul loewen

when he says, "I don't think we'll make the target. We'll aim for the grass." By this point there seems to be a wind blowing against us, preventing us from going forward. I look down and notice we're over the little airport, and beneath us is a wide tarmac of concrete. It looks less inviting than the gravel landing pad we want.

"Alright, we're not going to make the grass. Lift your legs up," we're fifty feet up now, and we both know we're hitting concrete. I look at the airport and see three people running full speed across the tarmac at us. I look over to my friend, who's landing first, and see them miss the target and hit the grass. The minute they land, the parachute buckles and the wind picks it up like a sail. Together, him and his instructor fall over and slide a few feet. Suddenly, the people running towards us make sense.

We hit the ground and, at the same instant, three pairs of hands grab us and, with their combined momentum, knock us over. As the parachute attempts to scrape us along the concrete, they hold us steady. We made it.

Believe it or not, there's a point to this story:

I've been in the clouds.

And they were rather disappointing.

And, apparently, heaven is not up there.

I say this because when people think about heaven they usually picture clouds. It's often depicted that way in movies and pop culture (and Cream Cheese commercials), so who can blame us? Besides, heaven is a hard concept to wrap our heads around, so using a symbol like clouds makes sense. The problem is, the symbol we used came to replace the thing itself.

If you were to think honestly (and avoid the answer you **know** you're supposed to give), what would your answer to this question be: If you were to wake tomorrow, and you could choose between being in your bed at home and living your normal life or being in heaven, which would you choose?

If you're honest with yourself, I'm guessing there's at least a part of you saying, "I like my life. I like my family. I like my friends. I've got stuff to do. I want my life."

Don't feel guilt about this.

There's a quote that says, "I know the joy here, I don't know the joy of heaven. I pick the joy I know."[2] This place we've got is good, scars and all. I laugh, cry, sing, dance (when no one's looking), and smile. I think there are two reasons for this:

Reason #1: We're afraid of dying.

Not so much afraid of death. When I think about **death** I think about heaven, and I think of no tears, no pain, being reunited with others, etc. But when I think about **dying** I picture all the ways it might happen, the date with Jeanette I might miss, or that I won't get to play Tickle Tackle later with my kids. I'm afraid I won't be able to say goodbye, or it will hurt like crazy and the pain will kill me. I'm afraid that, if I know I'm dying, I'll have an emotional crisis.

Reason #2: Heaven doesn't sound exciting.

First problem: We describe it as clouds. Here's the thing: if you Google clouds you might get more relaxed, but you won't get excited. In fact, that's exactly what you get if you Google heaven, too.

---

[2] I tried to find the person behind the quote, but failed. It's not mine, though.

paul loewen

Second problem: Clouds make it seem like it's "over there," which, if I turn it around, could be described as, "not here." There are a lot of things we like about "here," so being away from here scares or saddens us.

Third problem: I've heard heaven described as "A church service - forever." Now, church is great and all (I work in one), but even I wouldn't want to sit in a church service forever. Come to think of it, there's not much I'd want to do **forever**.

Fourth problem: For the most part, skydiving and bungee jumping, snorkeling and driving a racecar, laughing with friends and going to a concert, reading a book and cozying up by a fire, these things all sound better than the idea we have of heaven.

Because of these problems, we don't want to go there and we have a hard time telling other people about it because it's not easy to convince someone they should be excited when we're not excited.

Here's the thing: the problem isn't our excitement, it's our image. It's this picture we have of heaven that isn't helpful, and we need to get it out - quick!

We have this idea that faith is a little bit like getting on a rocket ship to an unknown (yet supposedly desirable) destination. We're leaving the earth behind, and we'll never see it again. It'll burn up when the sun explodes, or God destroys it, or we wreck it so much there's nothing left. Our destination is sort of known, but imaginative and mysterious. "It's great," we say, "better than anything you can imagine."

In Isaiah 65, Isaiah quotes God saying, "Look! I am creating new heavens and a new earth, and no one will even think about the old ones anymore." Cool, he's **re-creating** something that already exists. "The wolf and the lamb will feed together," he says later, painting this beautiful picture of a place of harmony and wholeness.[3]

The place God is creating is not a distant, mystical land. It's **this** earth, **this** place, re-created and made new. It's not a **where** question but a **when** question.

The problem with our traditional idea of heaven is it's about getting us some**where**, when the Bible's picture of heaven is about some**when**.

The world has evil in it. For as long as we can remember, there has always been war, poverty, injustice, sickness, pain, hatred, lust, envy, assault, jealousy, and malice. It's not a pretty place, and the presence of technology connecting the world means we are more aware of it than ever. These are some of the **negative** characteristics of earth.

---

[3] Wholeness is, perhaps, one of the best words to describe the Hebrew word **shalom**. It speaks about wholeness, peace, completeness, restoration, harmony, etc. We often translate it as "peace" in English, but it's so much more than that. It's not just the absence of fighting or war, it's the presence of something so much **greater**.

paul loewen

In contrast, we talk about heaven using words like this: joy, love, perfection,[4] happiness, peace, shalom, fulfillment, no crying, no pain, unity, loved ones, God, worship, holiness. These are wonderful words, and we say them with a longing as we look towards heaven (particularly as people age and get closer to death).

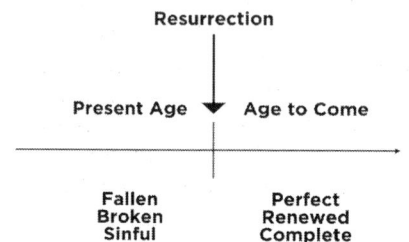

In Jesus' time, they viewed the world in terms of a timeline. They were in the "present age," which had the negative characteristics (and more) I listed above. One day, we'd move into the "age to come," which would replace all the garbage with all the good of heaven: joy, love, peace, etc. Basically, that age was the time when God would rule, wrong would be made right, and sorrows would be no more.[5]

The thing separating the "present age" from "the age to come" was **resurrection**. As in, when all those who died would come back to life to enter this awesome new future God had built. So the people of Jesus' time were watching for this glorious future, and were watching eagerly. Jesus spoke often about God's kingdom, and that it was coming soon, so people naturally got excited about the shift about to happen.

And then Jesus died.

And came back to life.

---

[4] The Junior Youth came up with "Stomach perfection," as in always having enough but not too much.

[5] That's a partial quote from "The Chronicles of Narnia," regarding Aslan. I just couldn't resist.

And, seemingly, nothing else happened. If resurrection was supposed to kickstart this whole "age-to-come" transformation, why was Jesus resurrected and no one else? Why didn't **his** resurrection change things?

Later on, Paul refers to Jesus' resurrection as the "first fruits" of a greater resurrection to come.[6] At harvest time, the first fruits were the first produce the farmers would bring off the field. They were a small taste and, more importantly, a promise the harvest would happen. To call Jesus' resurrection the "first fruits" was to say Jesus' resurrection guaranteed our own. It proved resurrection was possible, and ours was coming.

So, we're now in the problematic area between the "present age" and the "age to come." It's a conundrum, but the picture suddenly starts to become clearer. Throughout his ministry, Jesus said cryptic things like, "You'll see the kingdom of God come," and, "You won't die until you see the kingdom of God."[7] Problem is, those disciples later went on to die, and we're still not in the "age to come."

We're in the in-between.

This is the time when we still live in a fallen, broken world, but we experience and glimpse bits of the next one. So we have evil, misery, death, while also experiencing joy, elation, hope, miracles, and God's Spirit. This is what Jesus meant - the kingdom **had** started.

Someone, somewhere, decided to give this time period the name, "The Already but not Yet." Clever,

---

[6] 1 Corinthians 15:20.

[7] Matthew 16:28.

paul loewen

I know. And so now we've got this intermediate bubble, where the old hasn't ended and the new has started (but not in full).[8] Here we experience both the negative aspects of earth and the positive of heaven. Here we're stuck in this place where

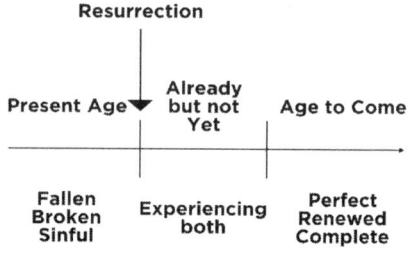

we want more but keep getting dragged down by the surrounding stuff.

So, the thing with heaven is it's still a matter of

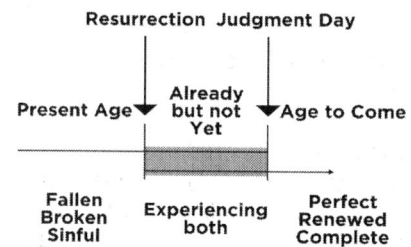

when, but the timeline has been pushed back. Now we can expect the "age to come" to start after Judgment Day, Paul tells us. This is the time when God decides to finally come and fold the earth back in on itself, and unfold it in a beautiful, re-created, renewed way.

In Revelation 21, we get a picture of this new heaven and new earth. It looks like this: "Then I saw a new heaven and a new earth, for the old heaven and the old earth had disappeared. And the sea[9] was also gone. And I saw the holy city, the new Jerusalem, coming down from God out of heaven like a bride beautifully dressed for her husband. I heard a loud

---

[8] Rather than one timeline with three stages, it's better to picture it as two timelines (present age and age to come) that overlap. We're in the part that overlaps.

[9] Sea, in that era, represented chaos. Also the same reason it shows up in Genesis 1 and has God "taming" it.

40

shout from the throne, saying, 'Look, God's home is now among his people! He will live with them, and they will be his people. God himself will be with them. He will wipe every tear from their eyes, and there will be no more death or sorrow or crying or pain. All these things will be gone forever."

That's a sweet image!

Take note of a few clues:

First, the city is coming **down**. We are not going up. There is no "away" to escape to.

Second, God Himself is coming down to be with us.

Third, the image is even better than the one in Isaiah (there was still death in that one). Now all the bad stuff is wiped away.

It keeps going in chapter 22, "Then the angel showed me a river with the water of life, clear as crystal, flowing from the throne of God and of the Lamb. It flowed down the center of the main street. On each side of the river grew a tree of life, bearing twelve crops of fruit, with a fresh crop each month. The leaves were used for medicine to heal the nations. No longer will there be a curse on anything. For the throne of God and of the Lamb will be there, and his servants will worship him. And they will see his face, and his name will be written on their foreheads. And there will be no night there - no need for lamps or sun - for the Lord God will shine on them. And they will reign for ever and ever."

Lots of signs to note here:

First, there is a lot of physical imagery: river, water, throne, street, tree, fruit. This goes back to when Jesus came back from the dead. If you remember, his disciples are locked in a house. Jesus shows up among them (sweet, he can go through walls!). And then he shows them his scars (even telling Thomas to touch them), to prove he is physically there (and not a ghost or spirit). Later, he shows up on the shore of the lake, eating breakfast. He couldn't say it louder: "I went through death and resurrection, and I'm different but still physical!" The Apostle Paul tries to put language to this in 1 Corinthians 15, but even he has a hard time.

Second, if you were wondering, that **is** the same tree as the garden of Eden. If you never noticed it before, Genesis has **two** trees. One is for life, the other is for knowledge. The one they weren't allowed to eat from was the knowledge one, so we can assume they could eat from the life one (presumably giving them immortality). Well, when God kicks them out of the garden He removes the tree of life, so unfortunately the immortality stopped. He took it away, possibly to protect us from the amount of evil immortal people would be capable of, and now He's giving it back!

Third, there is stuff to **do** in heaven. Here it's called "reigning," as in, "having control over." Jesus alludes to the fact some people will have bigger jobs than others in heaven.[10] So the idea that we'll be floating around endlessly with nothing to do is ludicrous.

So here's where we land:

Heaven is not made up of clouds.
Heaven is not a **where** but a **when**.
We're stuck in a middle age, between the old and new.
We experience the old, and get glimpses of the new.
That new age is both physical and different, including immortality.

---

[10] Matthew 19:28.

We'll have stuff to do in heaven.

So, rather than images of clouds, we should picture snowboarding down a sweet mountain with Jesus (and no chance of pain). We should imagine being able to run for miles without getting tired. We should imagine being able to pursue our hobbies and interests with unlimited free time and God to enjoy them with. We should take our best experiences on earth and multiply them by a thousand, not to try to get at what they **might** be like, but because this is what it **will** be like. We're heading back to the garden, back to freedom, back to the glorious world God intended for us - and it's even better this time around.

The crazy thing is Jesus' resurrection showed us heaven isn't distant from us, it is with us now, creeping into the present. The reality is **heaven is awesome** and **heaven starts now**;[11] we have a role to play in bringing it to earth, and we can choose to participate by joining in God's work to redeem the whole world through peace, justice, and love, and also by celebrating the laughter, joy, and happiness heaven has given us already.

---

[11] For a much deeper dive into this entire topic, take a look at N. T. Wright's "Surprised by Hope."

before
i go

4 the kiss of justice and mercy

Several years ago, a teenager was attacked by his classmates in North Kildonan on the way home from school. And it wasn't just fists; they used a hammer, and the boy was left with brain damage, fighting for his life in a hospital. It was a horrible story of bullying, of terrible tragedy and sadness. My friend, a nurse, took care of him. And while the media attention disappeared quickly, his care had to continue well beyond the spotlight.

For days, I pictured what I would have done if I had been driving or walking by. In this case, if I was driving, I pictured revving the engine and driving up the curb to knock the two boys off of him, somehow avoiding the boy on the ground. If I was walking, I pictured tackling them to the ground and fighting them until the police came.

I don't think it's abnormal to admit those inclinations, but the next part is harder. Disturbingly, in my imagination, I didn't want to stop hurting them. I didn't want to stop when they were on the ground and under control.

I'm not sure if you've ever pictured a situation like that (perhaps someone you love being hurt), but it's hard not to fantasize revenge. It hurts me to think about, and it hurts me to write about. For many of us, imagining the violence I just described might not be easy. I did my best to keep it as innocent as could be while also doing justice to the story.

Justice.

Justice is, like my story, the feeling rising up within us when there's pain and hurt and we want to set it straight. It's the part of us that wants to hurt them as much as they're hurting the boy. I don't blame you, and I don't blame myself.

In fact, the part of us crying for justice in this situation is from God. God cares deeply about justice, about right and wrong, about pain and oppression, about balancing and making things right. We inherited those traits from God, and our feelings (but not what we do with them) are built into us for a reason: to make things right, to make sure no one else is hurt the way that boy was. The same way we get ticked off at violence, or cry at injustice, or donate to relieve oppression, God hurts when we're hurt, when the world hurts.

Our moral compass is because of God.

Something in us knows it's not right, and it turns out it was put there by God: "[All] demonstrate that God's law is written in their hearts, for their own conscience and thoughts accuse them or tell them they are doing right." (Romans 2:15)

If you search Google for "justice," the first thing you get is weigh scales. We don't usually use scales like this anymore; our scales now just display a number or tell our phone how heavy we are. But back before digital readouts (or even the dials spinning  around) weigh scales were a more visual way of measuring. The scale was a teeter-totter, and you'd put a known weight on one side (a kilogram, for example) and then, if the scale balanced perfectly, you'd know your object also weighed a kilogram. If the scale was leaning one way or the other, you'd know your object was either lighter or heavier than a kilogram.

In the case of justice, the scales should be even. It means it is balanced. The first explanation is that, in court, you'd hear both sides of the story before making a decision. A second explanation, and a more common one when talking about justice in the Bible, is for the punishment to match the crime. Basically, if I steal one sheep, you don't get to take twenty of mine. If someone kills someone, you don't wipe out the murderer's entire family. It might sound crazy, but it's what people were prone to doing. You might have heard the law of, "An eye for an eye." People like to use it today to say, "Well, you killed someone, so we can kill you." That's partly the reasoning behind the death penalty. In reality, that verse was a **limiting** law. It was common back then for the revenge to be far **worse** than the original crime. God was saying to Israel that they weren't to wipe out an entire village because someone murdered someone. Instead, the punishment was to go **up to but not over** the damage of the crime. It was a radical concept back then, and we shouldn't use it to justify executing murderers today.

paul loewen

In something called "restorative justice," the idea is the punishment **relates** to the crime. If you break something, your punishment is to fix it (and possibly pay a fine, etc.). This has its limits (you can't fix murder), but the idea has been used in places today and has been seen to be more effective than putting people in jail.[1]

The reality is we want justice, because there's a lot of evil out there.

So we ask, what does God's justice look like? How can we balance justice and mercy? Is it even possible?

As a society, we love superhero movies. They come out all the time, and they're often the go-to for young people. I'm sure there are all kinds of psychological reasons for this, but I'll point out a few I've noticed:

1. They have abilities we don't have.
2. They're often ignored in their normal life, and we like the idea of being powerful and yet secretive.
3. We like that they beat up the bad guy/girl.[2]
4. We like that they save the good guy/girl.

Since 1995, they have been making more and more superhero movies. In 5 years (from 1995-1999) there were 6 superhero movies made. In the following 5

---

[1] It also takes a lot more work, which is why many countries just do the "easy" thing of putting people in jail. Restorative justice also often includes conversation between the criminal and the victim. In the case of a murder, this would be between the murderer and the victim's family. Obviously, both sides need to want to do this.

[2] I can't, off the top of my head, think of a movie with a female as the villain. However, I wanted to be gender inclusive.

years there were 16 made (2000-2004). The next 5 years brought 28. Then 23. And in the last two years alone we've had 13. We went from

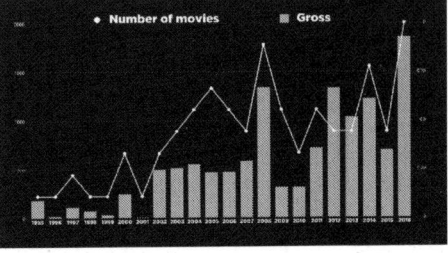

spending somewhere around $100 million on superhero movie tickets to $1.9 billion last year.

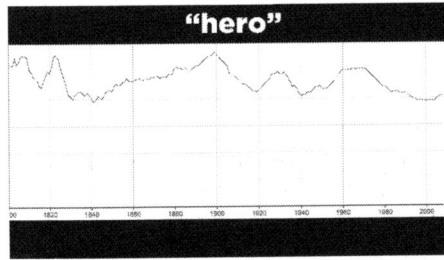

Heroes aren't new. Take a look at the chart - it's how often the word "hero" was used in books from the year 1800-2000.[3] But when we talk about heroes, we're usually talking about normal people doing cool stuff. Our interest in the word superhero, and this idea of beyond-normal abilities, is a recent trend. We've started using the word "superheroes" like crazy in the last forty years, and it doesn't seem like it's going away anytime soon.

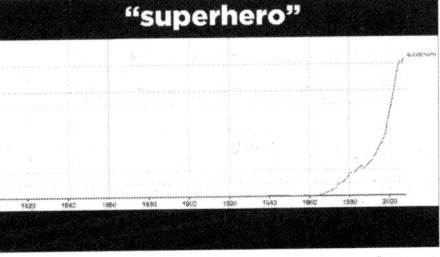

---

[3] If you've never heard of Google's N-Gram Viewer, it's fun to play with. Basically, Google will search all books in its database (they're trying to digitize every book in existence) for words and how often they're used. You can graph them, and see when words became common and then disappeared. https://books.google.com/ngrams

paul loewen

Maybe we're dazzled by strange abilities and sci-fi movies.

Or maybe we recognize something is missing within society, that our approach to justice isn't doing what it was supposed to do.

There's an irony about justice: we want it for others, but not for us. Specifically, we want God to finally **do something** about the evil in the world, but we want God to **show us mercy**.

We want God to give justice to **them** but not **us**.

We want God to give mercy to **us** but not **them**.

The reality is we can't have one without the other. Though it might make us uncomfortable, justice for everyone includes us. Mercy for everyone would include murderers, rapists, and terrorists.

Before we dive too deep, let's take a look at what the words mean.

Justice is based on what is morally right and fair.

Mercy is compassion or forgiveness shown toward someone we have the power[4] to punish or harm.

So let's go **all the way to mercy**, and show compassion and forgiveness from God's perspective.

The first emotion we might feel is overwhelming gratitude and happiness, as we realize all our mistakes have been washed away. Probably, the

---

[4] Maybe it should have been more obvious to me, but I found this part of the definition interesting. In other words, you can't have mercy for someone you can't have an impact on. This would include people in power over you, or people around the world.

more we've done wrong the more we'll be thankful.[5]

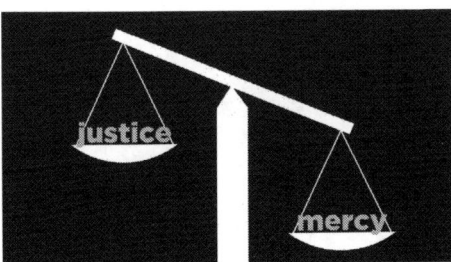

The moment it fades, the second emotion we might feel is concern. Are we forgiving all the evil people in the world? That's okay, I suppose, if we forgive them in our hearts but don't, you know, let them out into the world. The third feeling we might experience, if we realize true mercy goes further, is fear if we decide we're about to give them their freedom.

Going all the way to mercy is like a parent who ignores every time their kid lies, hits, or steals. It might mean they avoid the temporary temper tantrum that would come with parental discipline, but it's not helping in the long run. It's treating God like a vending machine when we've got a limitless credit card, expecting everything to turn out our way when we botch things up over and over again.

The result is a spoiled, greedy, and particularly unchanged individual and world. There's no forward progress, there's no movement or transformation (which God loves to do).

We want mercy all the time until we realize what that looks like.

So let's go the other way, **all the way over to justice**.

The first emotion we might feel is massive satisfaction, as we become aware of the punishment

---

5 Jesus has a real-life story and parable about this. Check out Luke 7:36-48.

all the criminals, murderers, rapists, and thieves will experience. It's an all-encompassing satisfaction, since we know it includes those whom the police never caught or those who were never put in jail because of lack of evidence. A win for all the good guys, right? The second emotion we 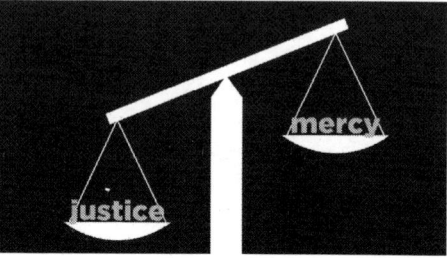 might feel is startling self-discovery as we realize, in our own ways, we do things deserving of punishment and/or justice. Maybe those aren't as big (on a social-impact scale) as the crimes listed above, but they're a big deal all the same. We lie, cheat, steal, lust, envy, betray, gossip, and insult. We do it to people we don't know, we do it to our friends, and we do it to our family. Often it's the ones closest to us who get hurt the most. The third emotion we might feel is a sense of guilt followed closely by fear. Fear because of the long list of wrongs I just mentioned, and if God is going to start punishing everyone (even if the punishment is based on how bad the offense was, we know we're not getting off easy) then that includes us.

Going all the way to justice is like a harsh judge or an unforgiving parent. Every moment is a lesson to be learned, pain to be felt, and a time for character to grow. It's like a terrible boss who just won't get off your back. It's like Santa making a naughty/nice list, measuring everything against a ridiculous standard and then giving Christmas presents (or coal) based on the mathematical outcome.

The result is a world filled with fear, condemnation (on ourselves and others), judgment, and paralysis because we are too scared to do anything out of fear we're going to sin. Again, it's a world with no transformation and no obvious way forward to grow as people.

The question becomes: is there a middle ground? Is there a way we can keep justice and mercy in balance?

In 1 Peter 2:24 we read this: "'He himself bore our sins' in his body on the cross, so that we might die to sins and live for righteousness." Now, if you're like me, the words at the beginning won't have much meaning for you. You'll hear phrases like, "Jesus died for our sins," and think, "Right, I've heard that all my life." Or maybe even, "Jesus put all our sins on his shoulders on the cross," which gives more clarity but still means little. How? Why? Did he **have** to?

A better question would be, "What **problem** did Jesus' death solve? **Why** did Jesus die?"

Jesus died to solve the problem of justice and mercy. It was an elegant (and creative) solution to the sin problem that sprang into existence when God allowed humans free will and the ability to disobey Him, as opposed to creating us all as robots.

Hebrews 9:28 says, "So Christ was sacrificed once to take away the sins of many."

Isaiah 53:5 says, "But he was pierced for our transgressions, he was crushed for our iniquities; the punishment that brought us peace was on him, and by his wounds we are healed."

If you think it sounds ludicrous God would give up His own son for the sake of our sins, you're not alone. In 1 Corinthians 1:18, Paul says, "For the message of the cross is foolishness to those who are perishing, but to us who are being saved it is the power of God." When Paul here says "perishing," he means those who don't believe in Jesus' sacrifice. When he says "foolishness," he's referring to the fact that, though we've grown accustomed to it because it's how we've talked about God since the day we started Sunday School, the idea of God dying on a cross is downright crazy.

Jesus paid for our sins on the cross, but how? And, the question I never thought to ask until recently, "Why did it matter so much that he was sinless?" Is that the key to understanding how his death could be the perfect mixture of justice and mercy?

Let's take a look at this by examining the possibilities:

The first question is: "Did Jesus sin?" As in, did he make mistakes that separated him from God? We'll look at the **sin** side of the equation first.

If Jesus sinned and didn't die, we're in a weird place. He wouldn't actually be the first person to head to heaven without dying - Elijah already did that,[6] and some think Enoch[7] did it, too. The thing is, we're not sitting here talking about them as the saviour of the world and the possible solution to the justice-mercy problem because they were normal people who lived normal lives. Sure, Elijah was a prophet (and did fantastic feats), but his life wasn't perfect and, if he did go to heaven in a whirlwind, it didn't dramatically change

---

[6] 2 Kings 2:1

[7] Genesis 5:24.

the world for the rest of us. So, Jesus sinning and not dying would put him in the camp of Elijah - an important prophet, but not the solution.

If Jesus sinned and died, then he **died for his own sin**. His death was the punishment he deserved for his sins throughout his life. The Bible makes it pretty clear that "the wages of sin is death," (Romans 6:23), and unfortunately it includes a single sin over an entire lifetime. Basically, God has set the bar so incredibly high **no one** can get to it on their own. Even the most perfect person you know acts imperfectly, outside of what God wants for them and for the world. So, if Jesus sinned and then died, even dying on a cross, the death would simply be a punishment for his own sin. We might remember him as a teacher and/or a prophet, but his death could not absolve **our** sins because he was already carrying **his** own. Justice would have been served - for him and only him.

If Jesus didn't sin and didn't die, no penalty was paid. He would have been a good or great teacher, an awesome example, but he wouldn't have been able to relate to us in any way. Since he didn't sin he didn't deserve to die, so no punishment was required. He could have gone floating into heaven without punishment, but now we'd still be stuck in the same situation. Justice may have been met for him (none was needed), but it would have been leaving us in our sin without hope.

If Jesus didn't sin and died, this is where it comes together. Because he didn't sin, the death was not for his own sins. Because he didn't deserve to die as punishment, he could take **other** sins onto his own shoulders - and not just the sins of a few, but the sins of **all**. He could take the punishment for all of our sins, all at once, and have the needs of justice be met.

paul loewen

The beautiful, magical outcome of his death is it served both the needs of **justice** and **mercy**. Justice because the punishment was served,

mercy because it was served by him instead of us.

The crazy power of the cross is it solved a seemingly paradoxical situation in an elegant and poignant way. It walks the line between justice and mercy and gives careful attention to both. It also shows us our incredible weakness and inability, and at the same time gives us a way up.

If we ask ourselves, "Did Jesus **have** to die?" we often feel bad if we don't immediately say, "Yes!" We hesitate because we're worried it makes God look like a mean God. Yet I don't think we have to answer, "Yes." The beauty of the cross is it shows a God who was **willing** to die, a God who cares deeply about our world's justice and, at the same time, won't leave us alone in our sins but shows mercy in the most incredible, powerful way.

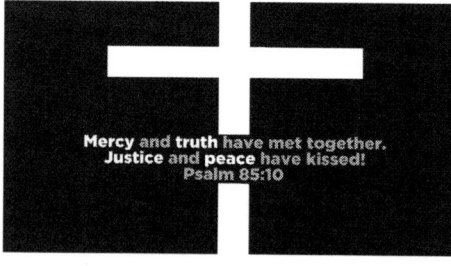

Mercy and **truth** have met together.
Justice and **peace** have kissed!
Psalm 85:10

If we look back at the weigh scales from the beginning of this chapter, we realize they look remarkably like a cross. Ironically, it's been staring us in the face the whole time. Psalm 85:10 says, "Mercy and truth have met together. Justice and peace have kissed!"

the kiss of justice and mercy

At the cross we find this beautiful intersection of two supposedly opposed ideas: the kiss of justice and mercy.

the tricycle of faith

You live in a crazy time. You probably hardly remember a world without the internet-in-the-palm-of-your-hand. I remember when we used to have arguments about which actor was in a movie - those end ten seconds later nowadays after a Google search. More information is helpful, but it can also be dangerous. Because you're the first generation to have so much access to information during the formative teenage years, new tools will need to be developed for making sense of it all.

You don't have to look far on the internet to find people who will think you're crazy for believing some dude who lived two thousand years ago has a say in how you live your life today, and what he did can possibly have significance for your life now and the life after you die. If you've gotten this far in this book, there **is** some craziness to you - a good kind of craziness.

Or maybe **you** feel like the person on the internet saying that, but you haven't had the guts to say it to your friends, family, or me. Or maybe you don't have the words to describe what you're thinking or feeling.

When it comes to those big questions and the big doubts, people who are defending the Christian faith are called **apologists** and the defense of the faith is called **apologetics**. That's what a large portion of this book is. Over the years I have read different apologists, and I've taken a lot of the traditional Sunday School answers and discarded them.

In this chapter, I'm not going to give Sunday School answers.

Instead, I want to give you tools.

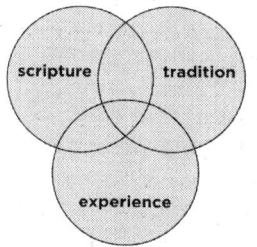

Let's start with three words: Scripture, tradition, and experience.[1] In some way, these words define how many Christians live their lives, make their decisions, and shape their future. They set the tone for discussions and/or arguments, and are the filters through which we pass almost everything. The way we think and act can be shaped by one, any combination of two, or all three of them. We're going to look at each of them, including strengths, challenges, and examples.

---

[1] The fact only one of those three words demands to be capitalized is interesting, and will be one of the mysteries we try to figure out in this chapter.

"That's what it says!" - You're the most likely to hear this from someone who operates **only** through the filter of **Scripture**.[2] Everything they do or believe has to be written about in the Bible.

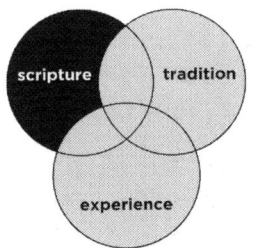

Strengths: The Bible is a remarkable document. It is both ancient (when it was written) and current (it speaks to today). It is an historical document, dating back to quite close to the stories it's telling. It is an eyewitness to history and gives us the most accurate picture of what happened then. It is also tried, tested, and true; over the centuries Christians have found it a meaningful source of knowledge and inspiration for their faith.

Challenges: It is tough to interpret the Bible (see chapter 2). It is also subject to bias, meaning you can probably find a basis for any side of your argument there. It is also only held as an authority by Christians, meaning using it as the basis for your argument with someone who doesn't hold it as true is useless. Lastly, it doesn't speak about a lot of the current questions (there is no verse about the internet, for instance). In cases like that, it gives us general principles and lets us work out the details in our current setting. This can lead to a lot of discussion, which can easily turn negative.

---

2 A filter works by eliminating everything other than what you want. Kind of like when you used those toys in the sand box to get rid of the sand and focus on the rocks.

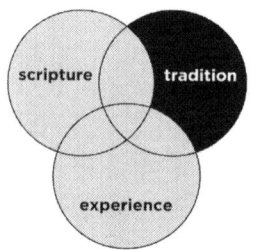

"That's what we've always done!" - You're most likely to hear this from someone who operates **only** through the filter of **tradition**. They're very aware of the past, and take church tradition, family tradition, or any other type of tradition, seriously.

Strengths: Traditions don't start without a reason, and they don't continue without a reason. They are time-proven, built on the past (so others have tried and found them working), and they help us remain focused. They keep us on track when we're prone to wandering after every flashy new trend. In the case of the church, they are also usually based on Scripture.

Challenges: Traditions can be built on top of incorrect understandings of Scripture, and are as subject to bias as Scripture. Often, they are shaped out of a specific culture in response to something. Eventually, when whatever triggered the response fades away, the tradition doesn't fade with it. Instead, it remains and is possibly elevated to an almost-equal status with the Scripture it was based on. Lastly, it can be difficult to separate tradition from Scripture. For instance, Mennonites are known for many stereotypes. Some of these include pacifism, a good work ethic, rollkuchen, thriftiness, and four-part harmony. Some of those are traditions (rollkuchen, four-part harmony), and some are theological convictions (pacifism, hard work, thriftiness). The more deeply connected one is to a tradition, the more difficult it becomes to make those distinctions.

"That just makes sense!" - You're most likely to hear this from someone who operates **only** through the filter of **experience**. They're

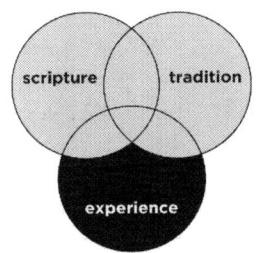

committed to having evidence for every belief, so if they haven't seen a miracle then miracles must not happen, and if a worldview can't be logically proven they're not going to follow it.

Strengths: This is more or less the scientific approach, and so it's likely to make good headway in conversations with non-Christians. If it all comes down to experience, it can be quantified, measured, photographed, or videoed. In some cases, it could even be repeated to prove it works or is true. It is also current, and can adapt quickly to changes or advancements in society.

Challenges: Try getting three people who witnessed the same car accident to agree on a coherent story; our memories are not as good as we think, and they are subject to the same biases that plague our understanding of Scripture or tradition. We are not as objective as we'd like to think, and have blind spots. They're called blind for a reason - we can't see them ourselves. Also, an experience one has needs to be believed by others to be held as truth. So while one person might witness a miracle, it's not likely to convince someone else. We're all skeptics when it comes to the experiences of others.

Now we turn to more complicated territory, by looking at the places where two of the three overlap. When it's just one, it's simple to draw out strengths and challenges. When there are two, it's murkier. So instead of strengths and challenges, I'll use examples showing, from my perspective, what it's like when one of the three is missing.

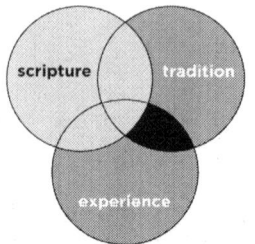

"I've felt God that way!" - This is something someone might say if they're connected to both the **tradition** and the **experience** they've had through tradition. Because it's linked with their memory, it doesn't have to be based in Scripture (but it can be).

Music, for many, lies in this category. Now, don't get me wrong - there's plenty of music in the Bible (take the Psalms, for instance). But music is particularly absent in the New Testament, and in the description of the way the church grew and reached out to people. Even in the Psalms, it's not the music but the words we remember today. However, music has been a part of church history for thousands of years, and it's a dynamic way to encounter God. It's entirely possible to have a significant spiritual encounter through music with no lyrics or completely unrelated lyrics as well. Because of the way it has been a part of church, and because of many significant encounters any one of us might have, music has become a staple in the church.

Baptism, and the way we go about it, is another staple. I'm not talking about how we baptize, but the significance of it. When Jesus' disciples baptized, it was much more of an instant reaction than it is today. It was for people who had just come to know Jesus and wanted to respond. However, over time, as the church grew and babies were born, baptism became separated because most within the church knew, right from a young age, who Jesus was. So it became a later marker of taking on an adult-like faith. At the same time, people often put down roots in a church. And so tying baptism to membership made sense. Couple this together with the fact church (and faith) has mostly been a communal experience, and the connection was reinforced. There's no biblical law forcing it to be this way, but we know how hard it is to be a Christian alone, and so we've linked the two.

Sermons, also, lie at this intersection of tradition and experience. They have been a part of the church since the beginning. Jesus preached them, and so did his disciples. On the other hand, structuring the church service around a 20-30 minute speech by one person didn't come from the Bible. It's not that the Bible says **not** to do it, it's just it never says this is the way we've **got** to do it. But over the centuries, with it always having been done a specific way, and with it being a good way of getting a message across, we've become okay with it.

Tradition and experience together are missing the element of Scripture. Without it, we are likely to elevate tradition to a divine status, or only rely on our experience and what we know works. This category faces many of the same challenges they each individually faced, sometimes countering each other but more often reinforcing each other until we feel like taking down one of these built-up institutions is like a slap in the face of Christianity itself.

"The apostles did it that way!" - This is what someone might say if they're connected to both **Scripture** and **tradition**, but

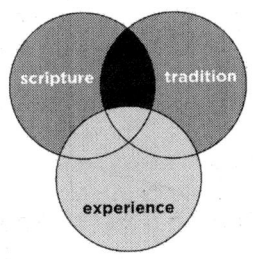

lacking in experience. If a belief is both affirmed in Scripture and tried, tested, and true, then they think it **must** be right, no matter our experience with it.

Decisions, and how we make them, can lie in this category. When Jeanette and I got this job at Douglas together, we were one of three applicants. They got us all in a room, and said they thought we would all do an excellent job. Then they pulled out three straws. One of them was shorter. In this case, whichever of us pulled the short straw would get the job. We were nervous! We went second, and the first person had clearly pulled a long one. So we were down to a 50/50 chance. Okay, just kidding. That's not at all true. We went through interviews, the leaders and congregation prayed and discussed and voted, and we were offered the job. You might have used a luck-based technique to pick teams or decide who gets the last piece of pizza, but there's no way anyone would use that to make a big decision, would they? Would they...? Believe it or not, the similar practice in the Bible is called "casting lots," and it was used regularly in the Old Testament. In the New Testament, since the number 12 was significant, the disciples needed to replace Judas and they chose two responsible, mature guys, and cast lots between them. So we have it in Scripture, and we have it in tradition. And yet, the Bible records, they stopped doing it. Rather than going around using an outdated system, the disciples recognized its limitations and decided it was time to put it back on the shelf.

Ritual laws, and whether or not we follow them, lie in this category. We're all familiar with the 10 Commandments, but little did you know there are 603 other rules and laws in the Old Testament! If you thought it was hard to avoid some of the Ten Commandments, just wait till you find out you've been breaking a bunch of the others! For instance, you can't wear clothes with mixed fibres,[3] your roof should have a parapet (like a railing),[4] and you should wear white to show you're happy.[5] Writer AJ Jacobs decided he would do his best to follow all 613 laws in the Old Testament for a year.[6] He found some laws made life difficult (like not trimming his beard[7]), while others made life more enjoyable (keeping the Sabbath[8] and wearing white[9]). What we have in these laws is Scripture and tradition coming together, but our experience[10] has taught us we no longer need to do what the ritual laws described.

Communal living, as another example of Scripture and tradition, is not common for Christians today. Those living in community are sometimes looked on strangely. I suppose when we go on retreats, Urban Plunges, SOARs, and Rivertons, we are doing a bit

---

[3] Leviticus 19:19.

[4] Deuteronomy 22:8.

[5] Ecclesiastes 9:8.

[6] The book is called, "The Year of Living Biblically," and is hilarious. CBS has bought the rights to do a TV show based on it, so it's possible you'll see it soon!

[7] Leviticus 19:27

[8] Exodus 20:8

[9] Ecclesiastes 9:8

[10] One of our experiences with regards to this is Jesus coming. In the Old Testament, most of the laws can fit in 2 categories: moral and ritual. Moral laws indicate what should or should not be done (the Ten Commandments is the obvious example). Ritual laws are what we do after we've broken the moral laws, like sacrifices, festivals, etc. Since Jesus, Christians have not kept the ritual laws (for the most part). We have our own now: baptism, communion, etc. The line between a ritual law and moral law isn't always clear. And there are certainly moral laws we have also disregarded today.

of communal living. It's seen as something to do for the young people, but no longer once we've "grown up," whatever that means. Communal living in the Bible stems from the commandments to love one another, share our resources, and from the example of the church in Acts 2, 4, and 5. It has existed in Scripture and tradition, but experiences with it are marred by jealousy, greed, and chaos. I have no doubt the experience of our inability to co-exist peacefully this way has led to it being a side-show of the Christian faith.

Scripture and tradition together are missing the element of experience. The message we've received has never properly been put into action, or, if it has, the experience did not translate in any positive way to the people experiencing it. In some cases (like casting lots), we look back on what is outdated with smugness in our superiority. In other cases (like communal living), we've pushed it aside because it isn't clean, tidy, or easy. In other other cases (like the ritual laws), we've recognized that they fit within a specific era but do not need to apply today.

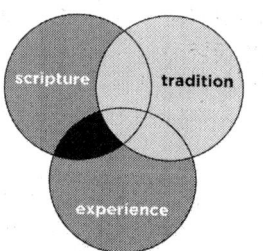

"Maybe God knew what He was doing!" - This is what someone might say as they connect with both **Scripture** and **experience** in the absence of tradition. This is when the light-bulb of inspiration turns on when you stumble across a poignant verse or story in the Bible, when insights suddenly click in your mind and life.

Social justice, for one, lies at the heart of this category. Maybe you've heard of the 1%, the fact the wealthiest 1% in the US earn nearly 25% of the money, or they control 40% of the wealth.[11] The top 20% (so, 1 in 5 people) have 83% of the wealth. The bottom 40% of the US have only 1% of the wealth. Those are crazy and frightening statistics. The world looking like this shouldn't surprise us; the ancient Israelites couldn't stop themselves from taking extra food, so why would we be able to? Well, for one, because God knew what He was doing. One of my favourite passages[12] in the Old Testament is regarding the Year of Jubilee in Leviticus 25:8-43, and it fights against this seemingly inherent nature of humans. To make a long passage short, it sets down rules about returning property, slaves, and letting the land rest. Over a fifty-year period there can be richer and poorer, and at the end of the fifty years the property is returned to its original owners. This does not prevent poor or rich, but it at least allows the poor to have a chance again. When Jesus rocks the house in Luke 4:14-21, he does so by claiming God's Jubilee (what the Leviticus passage was referring to) has started **now**. He says he has come to set the oppressed free, which is what Jubilee was supposed to do (we don't really know how much those laws were followed). So when we look at the system of complete imbalance today, we have to realize our church tradition has missed this boat completely - maybe God knew what He was doing all along!

Non-violent resistance is another way Scripture and experience come together, in the absence of a lot of church tradition. Many significant political and societal changes came about because people refused to fight back with their fists. Rather, Jesus'

---

[11] These and more here: http://inequality.org/wealth-inequality/

[12] I think I say this more frequently than I should. Still, it's a sweet passage.

message about turning the other cheek[13] and resisting without violence has led many Christians (and non-Christians) to stand up for what they believe. Take, for instance, the famous sit-ins of the African American population in the U.S. during the civil rights movement. They didn't happen to find themselves in the middle of a whites-only restaurant and decide suddenly they wouldn't leave. No, they set it up and made a plan, which grew out of the simple mindset changes would happen if they didn't fight back the traditional way. When this works, we can look back to the cross of Jesus and remember non-violent resistance is what led him there, which accomplished more than anyone would have guessed.

Feminism, also, clues us in to the fact that, despite our traditional ignorance of women's role in our faith, God knew what He was doing all along. If we take off the lenses making us read the Bible through today's equality, Jesus becomes an incredible beacon of light for women. He treats women with dignity, eating with them and respecting them. It's no accident the first people to testify to the empty tomb are women, whose testimony would normally not be taken seriously in a court back then. We've got good experience women are capable of leading, blessed with talents and gifts others, men included, might not have. We'd be fools to leave them out of church leadership, even though church tradition often has.

Scripture and experience are powerful together, often surpassing the mistakes of tradition. It's tough, because a lot of the time it includes overturning what has been understood to be correct (which is why it's become tradition). This isn't to say it's perfect, because experience and

---

[13] Not a message of submission, but one of clever disobedience. See the chapter on Jesus' Third Way.

Scripture can definitely get the interpretation and application wrong. Perhaps my three examples are more indicative of my concern for where the church has missed out on what Scripture was trying to do in the first place, and how our modern-day experiences connect with ancient words tradition has carried through to us.

And so we arrive at our **goal**. The last sentence of the above paragraph was not by accident. We wouldn't have the

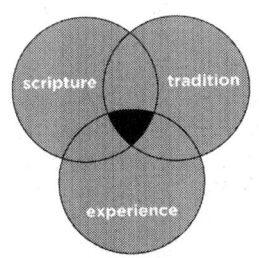

Scripture and the experience of it going "Aha!" in our minds if it wasn't for tradition bringing it here. It's beautiful when all three come together. Scripture, carried by tradition, can change our experience. Tradition, built on Scripture and experience, guides us. Experience, informed by Scripture and tradition, can give us the passion to grow in our faith. Our goal, then, is the beautiful inter-connectedness of the three aspects of our faith.

So, how do they interact?

It's optimistic and downright naive to think the three interact in a beautiful, balanced way. Instead, one almost always leads the other two.

Think about the image of a tricycle.[14] There are three wheels on a tricycle, and yet only one of them steers. Scripture, tradition, and experience are our

---

14 Rob Bell has a podcast, and on an episode with Richard Rohr they introduce the idea of this tricycle. I use it shamelessly, and also recommend that episode of his podcast. https://robbell.podbean.com/e/episode-86-richard-rohr-and-the-alternative-orthodoxy/

tricycle of faith. The next question is: **Which wheel leads the tricycle?** When we talked at youth I asked you two different questions and the answers were predictable.

First question: Which wheel **should** lead the tricycle?

Second question: Which wheel **does** lead the tricycle?

Nearly all of you felt obligated to answer the Sunday School response of **Scripture** for the first answer. As Christians, we feel this is our duty, and to say less would be to shrug off our faith completely. But when it came to the second question, almost everyone answered **experience**. Thank you for your honesty, because it is the first step to having your tricycle function well.

The most important takeaway is, honestly speaking, **experience** is the first wheel in our tricycle most of the time. Simply acknowledging this goes a long way to allowing the tricycle to function in anything other than a lopsided way.

No matter how much we want Scripture to be the front wheel, experience ends up there. Even those who truly hold Scripture as the primary guide in their lives are viewing Scripture through their own lens and cultural experience. We can't help it - how we understand the Bible is shaped by our lives, experiences, and biases. Welcome to being a human.

Acknowledging experience, not Scripture, acts as the front wheel lets us work within its limitations. It's only by recognizing we view Scripture this way that we can consider removing our bias or lens. We can then use our imaginations to see from the perspective of others, to see what it would look like if we had **their** experience.

Pretending Scripture is the front wheel cripples what we do.

When it comes to this tricycle, it's helpful to ask ourselves questions about the subject, decision, or issue:

1. Does Scripture talk about this? What does it say?
2. What has the church traditionally believed? How has it dealt with this?
3. Does my experience talk about this? What does it say?

We can look at each issue through these questions and see if they match up. If they don't, keep asking questions about why not.

If **Scripture** is the one left out, dig deeper into what that Scripture means. See if you're viewing it through your own lens, ask others what they see, consult your pastor or mentor. Scripture is complicated, and the task of understanding it should not be left to any individual.

If **tradition** is the one left out, remember the church has been wrong in the past. As Mennonites, we are part of a tradition that rebelled against the established church. Discern whether rebellion at this point is a necessary step. Some issues are worth fighting for, some are not.

If **experience** is the one left out, remember God is not interested in deceiving us. If what we see directly contradicts what we believe, something is off. Faith is belief in the absence of evidence, not belief despite the evidence.

paul loewen

As I said earlier, I have little intention of trying to get you to put Scripture first in everything in life. What I **am** trying to get you to understand is experience shapes our view of Scripture and tradition, and recognizing this tendency is the first step to a fully engaging and vibrant view of Scripture, tradition, and experience.

And we got to ride a tricycle.

before
i go
god is _____

We're going to start this chapter[1] off by doing a little exercise. Grab a pen or pencil, and spend a few minutes writing every word that comes to mind to finish this sentence: "God is _____." Write five, ten, or twenty answers in the blank space below, and flip the page when you're done.

_____

[1] This chapter was never a devo. Originally it was the opening and closing of chapter 5, but it distracted from the tricycle. I ended up deciding to write it and put it in because it was the perfect example of the tricycle in action. And then, on SOAR, this topic came up when we saw the pain of our world and had to ask, "Where is God in the brokenness?"

Now that you've written numerous options, think about them. If I said you had to narrow them to three, could you do it? Flip back to the other page, and think about it. When you have your three, write them in this space.

Now that you've got it down to three, we're going to take it further. I'm sure those three characteristics are all aspects of God, but, surely, one of them must lead the other three (just like our tricycle from last chapter). If one of them was the front wheel of God's tricycle (from your perspective), which one would it be? Take a minute or two to think it through, then write it in the blank space.

God is _____.

You might have the same word there as someone else, and maybe not. Your experience of God growing up will probably dictate what word you used. Though you wrote down numerous options, you were able to narrow it to one **core** characteristic of God. From your perspective, those other five (or ten or twenty) characteristics all, in some way, follow from this core characteristic. You could, then, say the characteristic you wrote is the **picture** of God you have.

How we **picture** God determines how we **respond**. If we see God as a judge, we will expect judgment from God and we ourselves will judge others for their sins. If we picture God as a vending machine, we will ask repeatedly without any thought of worship, service, or gratitude. If we picture God as a sandal-wearing rebel, we will look for injustice and cry out at oppression.

God is **good**. You may not have this attribute on your list, or maybe it made your top three, but the Bible reminds us of it repeatedly. We hear it in worship songs, too, and we repeat it back and forth to one another when things are going well. What about when things aren't going well, when bad things happen? When people suffer? For many, those questions define their image of God, which changes their response to God. So, let's look at that big question:

If God is good, why do people suffer?

I find we usually ask this question in two different ways.

The first way is completely **theoretical**. We see the pain people in the world feel, particularly those experiencing illness, poverty, hunger, and injustice. We get into saying, "Well, it's for the greater good." Really? Are millions of children around the world suffering because it's for the greater good? Are people dying at young ages because it's for the greater good? As a theoretical issue, all kinds of debates can be had and people can come to relatively comfortable conclusions allowing for evil in a world run by a loving and powerful God.

The second way the question is asked is when it becomes **personal**. It's no longer about the people over there, but it's now about us, or about someone close to us. I have no doubt we can all think of someone we know who has been affected by cancer, mental illness, tragedy, or more. Suffering doesn't care about borders or boundaries. We might feel **abandoned** by God, **betrayed** by God, or perhaps even **punished** by God. When we're hurting, no kind of logical jujitsu can rescue us. We might have heard the answers, but at this point they don't matter - we just want the suffering and pain to end. We desperately want an emotional and

77

personal answer to what is happening in our life - what caused it? Why did God give this to us? Do we deserve it? What do we have to do to make it go away?

This question has driven many committed Christians away from God, fueled debates between atheists and Christians, cut Christians down, and chipped away at their resolve to believe in a good God. When those beliefs collapse, some Christians cease to believe in a God at all. So are those our only options?[2] To either suffer through cliched answers or stop believing in God?

If God is good, why do people suffer?

Our answers fail us because we're asking the **wrong** question. In fact, I believe we should ask two questions.
1. Is God good?
2. Is God all-powerful?

We can answer with assurance, YES, to both questions. We know from Scripture, even if we don't always agree with it in our hearts and our emotions. Then why do people suffer? Well, we've circled back to the same question, and we realize the problem is the question itself!

Let's change the second question to what lies underneath: **"Is God in control?"**[3]

---

[2] You know I wouldn't have this chapter if they were :)

[3] Let me be clear here: I'm not taking power away from God. I'm separating **power**, which I here mean as the ability and capacity to do something (of which God has and always will have infinite), from **control**, which I here mean as manipulating every single occurrence in our world: blessings, miracles, global wars, deaths, down to which socks I wear in the morning.

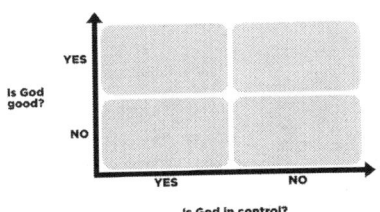

Most Christians would seriously hesitate to answer the question with any response other than a resounding YES. Take a look at the chart. "Is God in control?" is along the bottom, with YES and NO answers. "Is God good?" is along the left side, with YES and NO answers.

Square 1: We'll start with the top-left corner, the YES and YES square. If we're answering in Sunday School, this is where we

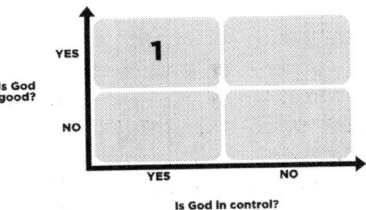

would think our answer should end up. What does a world in which God is good and God is in control look like? It looks like **utopia**, perfection, and wholeness. In this kind of world, where a good God always gets His way, we'd get the paradise God dreamed up. To put a label on it, I think we'd have to call it "Heaven." Though I think the Garden of Eden, in the beginning of creation, gets extremely close to this, it is slightly different because it was clear Adam and Eve were given a choice to disobey. If we want a perfect world with no chance of any suffering, we need to remove the chance of evil, which means removing our choice to disobey. This is the world of the YES and YES, the heaven up in the top-left corner. If the "correct" answers to my two questions are YES and YES, then we should find we live in square 1. Take a look around: it's clear we don't.[4]

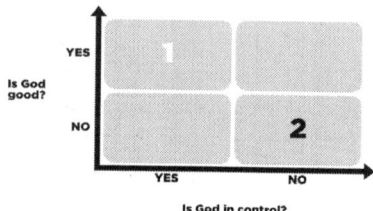

Square 2: We're going to move next to the opposite square, the NO and NO. In this square, God is not good and God is not in control. This is a rather **bleak** world. It's a world with no hope, no sense of justice or basis for morality, and it leaves the world feeling ultimately pointless. At first glance, there is no real mention of this worldview in the Bible. But if you take a deeper look, you'll realize even though it's not **in** Israel it is **surrounding** them. Many of the neighboring nations, like Egypt or Babylon, had a theology describing many gods, most of which were powerful over only a certain domain, and even then they were temperamental, moody, vengeful, and angry. Their gods were not necessarily good, and they certainly were not in control (they were too busy having their own wars, some of which spilled out into the human realm). This is not a world we'd want to have, nor is it the world we believe exists.

So far we've seen the two polar opposites: we've seen a joy-filled utopia, and a hopelessly bleak existence. Our world as I observe it does not fall into either of these categories. And so we move to the left.

---

[4] If your response to this is, "But God's got a plan we can't see!" I hear you, and more on that in square 3.

Square 3: In this square, we answer God is in control, but God is not good. There are some good characteristics of this world:

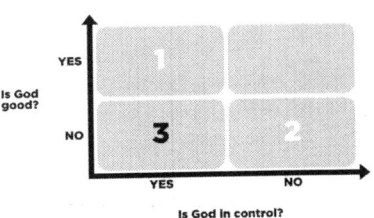

security, predictability, control. Since an all-powerful being is in control, we can expect it to be consistent. We would expect an orderly world, a world in which things make sense and have an explanation. But I think we'd also see a world plagued with **fear**, and a world in turmoil. Because if God is all-powerful and in control, yet not good, we'd be looking over our shoulders, we'd be watching our back, we'd be shaking with fear every moment we did something we knew God didn't like.[5] In many ways, this worldview represents much of what we see in the Old Testament. It is a predictable and known world, but it is a world with not much hope, a world defined by **fear of** rather than **love for** God. Many Christians today believe in a God like this.

With this worldview, we might say, "God is always in control," or "Don't worry, God's got a plan." We say this to minimize the hurt from suffering and tragedy, because we take comfort in the fact God, some all-powerful being, is in control. The problem we run into is, from our perspective,[6] what we call

---

[5] Also kind of what it's like to believe in a Santa keeping a list of naughty and nice.

[6] Yes, our perspective is limited. However, we are created in God's image and have, built into us, the knowledge of what's right and wrong (Jeremiah 31:33). If something that God is supposedly doing goes against what we **know** is wrong, we're left with the logical conclusion: either God did something evil, or God didn't do it.

paul loewen

God's plan doesn't always look good. In fact, sometimes God looks downright mean and vengeful. Scripture and tradition are both clear on this, though - we have a good God. We also have a God with unlimited amounts of power. Our beliefs exist in the top-left square, the YES and YES square.

But our reality doesn't exist in square 3.

Since we **know** God is good and God is in control, we do our best to finagle our way out of the situation. We say, "It's for the greater good." Basically, we're saying, "God knows the good we'll ultimately get to because of this suffering we're going through is better by far than the good we could have if God took away our suffering right now." We admit we are limited in our scope of the universe and use metaphors of going through the pain of childbirth to the joy of having children, the pain of exercising to result in the build-up of muscles. While all we can see is the short-term pain and the short-term gain, God apparently sees beyond these to the long-term good and knows the long-term good far outweighs the pain we're experiencing and, in fact, the long-term good will be far **better** because it wasn't just handed to us on a silver platter but was, instead, a process of transformation including some pain.

One of C.S. Lewis' most famous quotes is from his book "The Problem of Pain," in which he says, "God whispers to us in our pleasures, speaks in our conscience, but shouts in our pains: it is his megaphone to rouse a deaf world." It is true character transformation and depth of faith grows by leaps and bounds through suffering and pain - but it just hurts **so** much. Unfortunately, it is also true transformation is only really visible once we have gone **through** the pain.[7] When it comes to long-term versus short-term, most are more than willing to give up the character transformation for the relief of the pain. Though this explanation works, it still leaves us in the bottom-left square, a square in which our question of God's goodness is answered in a way not aligning with Scripture. We cannot reconcile a good God with Him actually **inflicting** pain on us (because if He is ultimately in control at every step of the way then we are left with only one option). If God is in control and pain exists, then God causing pain is the logical conclusion we come to. Whether or not it's for a long-term benefit, it still seriously challenges our understanding of God's goodness.

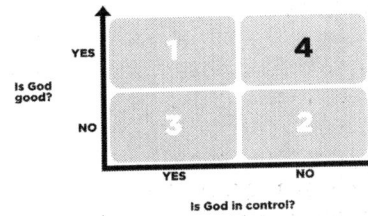

Square 4: So we move on to the last square, the one in the upper-right corner. In this square, we say God is good but not in control.

My immediate response to this square is "Uh-oh." If God's not in control, what's going to happen? Is our world going to fall apart? What would a world like this look like? This would be a world plagued with an **up-and-down** existence. It would be a world experiencing **hope** amidst **turmoil** and **pain**. It would be a world, essentially, entrenched in a battle. To put it simply, when I look around, this is what I see. **This is our world, our earth.**

When tragedy strikes, most people use God's control as a method of **comfort**. It brings them peace. I don't think this upper-right corner robs us of **peace**. To me, it gives a much deeper and richer

---

[7] Which is why, generally, it is a bad idea to say that to someone who is currently still in the midst of it.

peace. Though we may want to believe God is good and God is in control (square 1), when tragedy strikes us the first belief we usually let go of is God's goodness, reverting back to the human desire to always be in control. Not perhaps, saying God isn't good, but we are saying we don't understand what good means, that God has a different and more long-range perspective on good than we do. This isn't untrue. God does, of course, have a better understanding of what will benefit us in the long-term. How we express this belief changes our reaction to it - is God **giving** us the difficult times, or simply **letting** us have them? If He's giving, we're down in the bottom-left. If He's letting, we're up in the top-right. It is perfectly biblical and true to say God is good and God is all-powerful.[8] It is not biblical to say God causes suffering, but it **is** biblical to say God **allows** suffering. It **is** biblical to say God isn't always in control, and God doesn't always get what God wants.[9]

Like all problems, the problem of pain and suffering can be traced to a root cause. In the story of creation we read in Genesis,[10] we realize:

First, God created the freedom to disobey. Right from the beginning, He created a system out of His control. In the Genesis creation story, God made

---

[8] Don't get confused by the language switch. I did not say God is in control.

[9] Based on Scripture, if I had to summarize my understanding of what God wants, it would be something like this: God wants all humanity and creation to **choose** to be restored to Him through the death and resurrection of his son, Jesus. God wants community, shalom, peace, and happiness for all people.

[10] Genesis 1-3 says so much about our world, even if it was never intended to be a scientific explanation for how the world came to be. It talks about origins, intentions, purposes, challenges, and moves us in the direction of the solution.

space for freedom by planting a tree and telling Adam and Eve not to eat from it.[11] If He'd planted the tree but manipulated Adam and Eve to not eat from it, it would have been no different than not planting the tree in the first place.

Second, the first problem wasn't Adam and Eve's taking of the fruit, it was the serpent's deception about God's character. The first move Satan made was **question the goodness of God**. He manipulated the circumstances to indicate God didn't have their **best** interests at heart, that God was less than good because He was holding back from Adam and Eve. Adam and Eve were experiencing the benefits of the YES and YES square, but Satan pushed them into the bottom-left square by questioning God's goodness.

So they had a faulty **picture** of God and it led them to **respond** poorly, and sometimes we do, too. The image of God we **should** have is in the upper-right corner, but we are humans and, unfortunately, sometimes slip into the supposed comfort of the bottom-left corner. It's understandable, really. When things go wrong we want to have a sense they are under control and **someone** is watching over us. We'd rather give up believing in a good God and hang onto the safety and security of a controlling God.

If this picture Adam and Eve received, the same we often slip into, is inadequate and wrong, where do we turn to look for the real picture?

We could turn to the Old Testament. There we find an image of God seeming to match up with the bottom-left corner, an image where God is in control - sometimes incredibly so - and yet does not

---

[11] The tree represents the choice humanity has to disobey, whether Adam and Eve are real historical figures or not.

always seem good. I am sure the surrounding nations would argue that our God is not a good God at all. A powerful God, yes - they seemed to cower in fear at every turn - but they would seriously question the Israelites' claim that He was good. I will not be the first to admit I struggle with this image of God. Here there is no easy answer. We cannot wipe away what is written in Scripture, but we find it hard to reconcile with what we understand God to be. If Israel's surrounding neighbors had a view of the gods fitting into the bottom-right corner, then it was already a move in a better direction for the Israelites to have a view fitting in the bottom-left. It seems like the stories we read from the Old Testament have a strong bottom-left inclination. What I mean is, they **interpreted** every event, whether it be cause and effect, a natural disaster, a disease, plague, or even a war - as directly controlled by God. Since they held this **worldview**, they used appropriate language to describe the events. In the end, all it does is perpetuate that worldview.

I think we, as modern-day Christians, often turn to the Old Testament. We want a powerful and in-control God, and we take comfort in those beliefs. As I said, we'd rather follow a God that is not good than a God that is not in control, a God who doesn't get what He wants. But we have one more place to look: Jesus.

Jesus is our most accurate image of God, because he carries in himself God's word made flesh.[12] In John 14, Jesus says, "If you have seen me you have seen the father." Bold statement.

If Jesus is the representation of God the Father we should be looking at and holding in our minds, how does Jesus **respond** to suffering? Does Jesus point

---

[12] John 1.

the direction many Christians tend to point: God causes suffering to teach us a lesson, to punish us, to test us?

In John 5, Jesus meets an invalid at the pool who had been suffering for 38 years. He doesn't give him the pat answers we often say to ourselves and to others.

In John 9, Jesus meets a man who was born blind. The disciples ask Jesus the same question we have on our minds: "Jesus, whose fault is it he is blind? Did he sin, or his parents?"[13] Jesus dances around the question. "This has happened so that the power of God could be shown in his life." They want to know about **cause**, but Jesus moves immediately to **purpose** and **action**.[14]

In Luke 13, Jesus is confronted by two tragedies. In the first, some Galileans had been murdered. In the second, a tower in Siloam fell and killed eighteen

---

[13] My paraphrase.

[14] The Greek here is complicated. Since there was no punctuation, the interpreters had to take educated leaps. The way it is commonly worded makes it look like God caused the suffering for the purpose of its eventual healing (on this day). The key words are, "so that..." Dr. Thomas Constable has said it would be better translated, "But that the works of God might be displayed in him, we must work the works of Him who sent Me as long as it is day." In this translation, it doesn't talk about cause whatsoever (God or otherwise). The "so that" refers to the performing of the miracle, rather than the cause of his blindness. Writing Dr. Constable's translation a simpler way might look like this: "We need to do God's work so that God's power can be shown." If this is an interpretive option, we can look at the rest of Jesus' responses to pain to get a good idea of what he might have said. Jesus did not perpetuate the belief that God caused any of the sickness, disease, or suffering he encountered, leading me to believe it was more within Jesus' character and worldview to say something like Dr. Constable says he could have.

men. There are several possible causes: first, humans commit murder. Second, either a natural disaster like an earthquake could have knocked over the tower, or simply poor design and construction led to the mistakes. Jesus uses the moment to confront the prevailing worldview of God being behind the murders and tower's collapse. Since they had a controlling viewpoint of God, the people were assuming those suffering had done something to deserve their fate. Jesus responds with a firm "No!"

I could continue. I could go through the gospels and find more and more examples of how Jesus responds to people suffering. As I walk my way through the story of Jesus and look at the interactions he had with those suffering, there is one word coming to mind: **compassion**. When confronted with suffering, Jesus never blamed God. He never even excused God. He never said God had anything to do with the suffering. Instead, Jesus felt compassion. He empathized with those who were hurting. In some circumstances, it was his emotional response that led him to **action**.

In the story of Lazarus we see one of the most powerful examples of Jesus' response to suffering. In this case, the suffering was intense: the death of someone at a young age. Jesus' friend Lazarus became sick and died. In response, Jesus came to comfort Mary and wept with her. They then journeyed to the tomb, and Jesus felt another great wave of emotion come over him. In response, he raised Lazarus from the dead. He didn't try to philosophize Lazarus' death, he didn't write a nice, neat poem about it.

This example is typical of Jesus. When Jesus encounters suffering, he generally reacts in two ways. First, he responds **emotionally**. In the case of Lazarus his response was tears, in other cases it was compassion and mercy for those hurting. Second, he **does something** about it. He heals the person, raises them from the dead, restores them to community, touches them. He is not content to let suffering be. If God wanted people to suffer and if God put people **in** suffering, Jesus wouldn't have worked so hard, including going to his own death, to end it. He makes it obvious - God's role in suffering is to comfort and then bring suffering to an end.

Back to the original idea: our **picture** of God determines how we **respond**.

If we think God is **causing** everything, we are likely to look for reasons and/or give cliche statements like, "God wanted another flower for His garden,"[15] when someone young passes away. Really? God could have made a flower from nothing - He didn't have to end someone's life tragically!

If we admit God **allows** suffering because of the freedom He gave us,[16] we recognize we live in a messy, fallen world, but serve a wonderful God. He cares so much about this world He was willing to send His own son into it for it.

Rather than God being always in control and somehow less than good, we can come to understand God **is** good, and yet God chooses to limit the use of His power at times so we can have freedom. We live in a fallen world, and sometimes

---

[15] Yep, I've heard it said about a young person's death.

[16] This freedom is most obviously characterized by the choice to disobey He gave Adam and Eve. Why would God let Himself go through the pain of being rejected, of letting His most-prized creation and image bearers suffer, and of sacrificing Himself? It would have been much simpler to never give a choice if that freedom wasn't going to be a continuing trend in His creation.

God is successful, sometimes He is not. In order for us to have free choice, in order for us to be able to choose to turn to God or turn away from God, allowing the possibility of failure is the way it has to be.

It might mean we go through suffering, suffering that, I admit, all my philosophical and logical explanations won't end. In the midst of suffering, we don't want answers or lessons[17] - we want the pain to end. The good news is we can take confidence in knowing when Jesus was confronted with people who were suffering he didn't ask what they were learning from it. Instead, he felt compassion for them, stopped the pain, removed the suffering, and then restored the person to community and life.

We don't have a controlling God who inflicts suffering on us, we have a God who gives us free will, suffers with us, and asks us to join in removing suffering, because God is **good**.

---

[17] And we certainly don't want people to try to give them to us (see the book of Job in the Bible). Please don't read this chapter to someone going through suffering. Just be with them.

before
i go

god's game plan for you

There's an old tried-and-failed method of making decisions that, I'm pretty sure, many Christians have done (but aren't willing to admit they've done).

It goes like this: take your Bible, preferably a hardcover one that's been used a decent amount so the pages aren't sticking to each other, and stand it up on its spine. Then, like using a magic 8-ball, ask a YES/NO question. "Should I go to school in California?" Or maybe, "Will _(insert name of crush)_ say yes if I ask them out?"

Then let the Bible open and fall flat. If it lands in the Old Testament, it's one answer. If it lands in the New Testament, it's the other. The key to having this work is making sure the answer you **want** God to pick is the Old Testament, since it's significantly longer.

This isn't different from casting lots or rolling dice to make decisions. It would sometimes be nice if decisions were that simple. More often than not, however, they aren't. All those techniques do is reveal our true desires by showing us how we'd react if someone (or something) made the decision for us.

We make decisions in different ways.

- Some of us are pro/con people. We write the positives and the negatives about a certain decision, and see how they stack up. If we're technical, we even decide how big a deal each of them are, and create a point system. This can clarify decisions, but can also be a burden.
- Some of us will seek wisdom from those around us. We ask friends or family what they think we should decide. If we're not careful, we can paralyze ourselves for too long, asking others what **they** would do when it really matters what **we** should do.
- Some of us will be logical, making decisions based on past experiences, current situations, and what makes the most long-term financial, emotional, or mental sense.
- Some of us will rely heavily on emotion, going with what **feels** right.
- Some of us will, like mentioned at the beginning, leave it to chance, tossing a coin or rolling a dice.
- And, depending on the size of the decision, some of us will pray, seeking God's wisdom on the situation. The twist here is, unless we hear from God directly, God's wisdom is often displayed in some of the other ways above (advice from friends, logic, emotions, etc.).

For the little decisions (like what socks to wear in the morning) we're usually comfortable skipping many of the steps above, and going with whatever feels snuggly and bright. For the big decisions, we sometimes get stuck as we fret over the future. Our socks won't change much of our future. Who we marry will. When we throw God into the mix, there's often fear and misgiving added, because we don't want to step **outside** of what God wants for our life.

When the early church got going, it wasn't vastly different from the religion it was within, Judaism. In many ways, it was like a section of the church deciding it would add one more layer to its thinking then keep going. The early Christians **were** Jews, and weren't even called "Christians" until later.[1] They followed Jewish law, participated in Jewish festivals and rituals, and were seen as a sect (short for "section") within Judaism.

But the early church didn't stop there.

It grew to include people who hadn't originally belonged to Judaism. These people were called **Gentiles**. The original Christians started to ask: what do we **do** with these people? Do they need to be circumcised? Do the old traditions and rituals apply to them? To be a Christian do they **also** have to be a Jew?

In Acts 15, we read the outworking of this issue, and it's fascinating to see the way the church functioned. First, a group started teaching these new believers they **also** had to become Jews. Paul and Barnabas debated this fact, and were appointed to go to Jerusalem to figure it out. The most traditional members of the church were adamant the new believers become Jews as well, and so an organized debate began.

---

[1] Acts 11:26.

Finally, Peter made a few points.[2] First, it was God who determined the Gentiles **also** should hear the good news of Jesus. Second, God accepted them by giving them the Holy Spirit. Third, it's by grace, not the law, they are saved.

Afterwards, Paul and Barnabas started explaining the way in which the lives of these Gentiles had changed, and the miracles taking place. Then James jumped in and quoted the Old Testament, saying, "the rest of mankind may seek the Lord, even all the Gentiles who bear my name."[3]

The point became that the original Christians shouldn't make it difficult for these new believers, but focus on four important rules: don't eat food that was sacrificed to idols, don't be sexually immoral, don't eat the meat of strangled animals, and don't eat blood.

The church in Jerusalem then chose a group to head back to the original city to put this issue to rest. They wrote a letter, detailing what they believed was important. They sent a few of them back, and encouraged the church to keep on growing.

There are a few tips here about making decisions.

First, they had a group **discussion**. They sought each other out for advice. They didn't make the decision alone.

Second, they went to **Scripture**. There they found evidence God could work through people other than the Jews.

---

[2] Acts 15:7-11.

[3] It's a loose quote of Amos 9.

Third, they felt guided by the **Holy Spirit**. The church had previously (at the beginning of Acts) made a critical decision through the use of "lots," which was basically like picking straws. After that moment, they experienced God's Spirit coming to live inside of them, and they decided casting lots was no longer the way to make decisions.

Fourth, and finally, they trusted their **experience**: it was clear God had given these believers the Holy Spirit, and so who were they to stop what they saw with their own eyes?

When it comes to making big decisions in step with God's will, this story in Acts is a great place to start. It's not a prototype we have to follow rigidly, but it's an example we can draw inspiration from.

God's will is a phrase thrown around frequently in the Christian community, often to its own damage: if God's will is so incredibly important for us, why is it so difficult to find?

The reality is it's not nearly as difficult to find nor as scary to follow as many believe.

blueprint

game plan

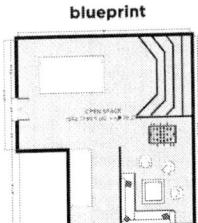

A **blueprint**[4] is a set of plans a builder or designer has for a building. It is intended to be followed as closely as possible, often with measurements down to 1/8th of an inch. It shows which wall goes where, and what each room is for. If you don't follow the blueprint,

---

4 The blueprint and game plan image is shamelessly borrowed from Larry Osborne's fantastic book, "Ten Dumb Things Smart Christians Believe."

the consequences could be disastrous. A wall might collapse, the roof might cave in, or maybe your entire house will sink. Not a good situation. The best course with a blueprint is to triple check to follow it as closely as possible.

A **game plan** is something a coach would draft before a big game, with plenty of options and variables. It might include a few hundred possible plays. The way a team will play is different if they're down with 5 minutes to go than if they're up halfway through. If your star player is out, you'll be forced to adapt. Game plans are inherently flexible, and allow for creativity.

A frequent comfort for many Christians is the belief God has a blueprint for their lives. This can lead to fantastically difficult situations. What if we mess the blueprint up? Are crime, sickness, and death part of the blueprint?

Seeing God's will as a blueprint for our lives acts as a crutch for vibrant faith.

Rather than focusing on love, justice, and mercy, we focus on whom to marry, where to go to school, and whether to pursue this career or that career.

Seeing God's will as a game plan is often scarier because it's not concrete, because it's fluid and flexible, because it seems to challenge the idea God has ultimate control.

Instead of spending our time stressing about the details, we can live our lives confidently, knowing God cares deeply about **who we are** more than the specifics. God's will is about **who you become**, not whom you marry or where you work. Now, before you start stressing about it, I'm not saying God doesn't care who you marry or where you work. I'm just saying God cares **more** about the **kind** of spouse or employee you are than the **specific** person you marry or the specific place you work.[5]

If we spend our lives searching for what God has designed specifically for us, we may be wasting valuable time. It's not that God can't speak into our lives and/or give us specific tasks, but the Biblical example is that, for those who had a specific mission or task, it was **clear**. Moses wasn't wandering around asking God what to do; God dropped a miraculously burning bush in front of him. For every Moses with a specific task, there were roughly 2 million Israelites without. Odds are, we are the Israelites.

And it's okay God doesn't have a specific path for us. The beautiful reality is God built choice into the fabric of the world. Now this isn't to say God doesn't care what we do - He absolutely does. But God makes it clear in multiple places that what He cares about is the **way** we live our lives. This includes the Ten Commandments, and it's echoed in Micah 6:8 where it says, "act justly, love mercy, walk humbly." Jesus nails it down into two ideas: "love God and love others." Other passages in the Bible

---

[5] People like to think the idea of a soulmate is romantic. Really? The fact you were destined only for one person out of 7 billion, you had no choice in the matter, is romantic? Rather, it's quite romantic that, day in and day out, you choose to spend your life with one person. I'm not saying you can marry anyone and it'll work out - but we, as people made in God's image, have free will in our lives. Besides the fact it's actually unromantic, it's statistically crazy: what are the odds, with 7 billion people on the earth (most of whom we'll never meet) you'd ever cross paths with your soulmate, and, especially, your interaction would be anything more than seeing them in a bus window as they drive by? The soulmate idea also leads to the dangerous scenario where, the minute there's discontent in a marriage, the person wonders if they missed out and their soulmate is still out there. Rather, they should spend the time making their spouse their soulmate, day in and day out.

paul loewen

add specifics, describing what that might look like on a day-to-day basis, but the gist is God has given us a task: love God and love others. Within those boundaries, our lives are relatively blank slates.

What can we do, then? We can live out great lives, following Jesus' example of seeking justice, being compassionate, 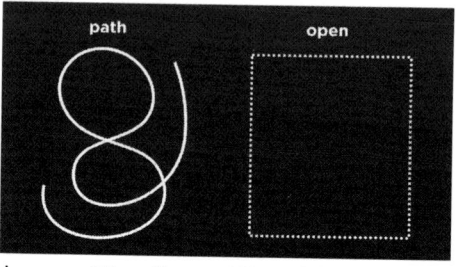 and sharing God's love with others. The difference comes down to the question of whether we're supposed to follow a **specific path** or work within a set of **boundaries**.

If you're walking through dense woods, a path makes the most sense. It keeps you from tumbling down embankments, getting snagged in branches, and falling into lakes. It turns left, zigs right, jogs up, drops down, and maybe even circles back around. But what it doesn't give you is freedom of choice.

God's will for your life is more like an open field with a fence or boundary running around it. God makes it clear there are dangers we should avoid in life. These boundaries are there because the actions are destructive to others, society, and ourselves. If we're not doing those things, we can zig left and zag right. We can jump in the lake and swim across if we don't want to walk around. We can climb the hill straight or take switchbacks to make it to the top (or avoid the hill altogether!).

When it comes down to it, God **does have** a specific will for your life: love God and love others. That's the end of it. **God cares more about who you are than what you do.** Our job is not to **find** something that takes us decades of decisions and prayer, as if

God has hidden it from us, but to **become** someone, someone made in God's image and following Jesus' example.

Our church has a connection with a missionary in Winnipeg's West End named Jamie Arpin-Ricci. Some of you have met him, and maybe some of you remember when he (or his wife, Kim) spoke at our church. Years ago, he shared how he ended up doing what he does. He grew up thinking he would take over the family business, but felt an unexplainable call to get into ministry. The two options were complete opposites: the family business was safe, predictable, and focused on achievement and success. The ministry option was dangerous, unpredictable, and focused on people.

Caught in the fork of two very different options, Jamie asked God what God wanted him to do. He heard God say, "If you follow in your family's footsteps, you will have all the good things you hope for and I will bless that. Or you can have my best for you and follow my calling into ministry."

Maybe you're thinking about your future, maybe you haven't started thinking about it yet. You might have options all over the spectrum: being a doctor, cleaning offices for a living, or being a missionary. All of those are great options, and the reality is God cares more about what **kind** of doctor, office cleaner, or missionary you are.[6]

When it comes to making decisions, we can follow the example I started with in Acts. We gather in

---

[6] I say this with the exception that if you are specifically called to something, you will know. We like to think the Bible shows everyone being called to a specific path, but it covers thousands of years of history and millions of people, and yet we can name many of the ones with specific futures. Even in those cases, God waited for a response.

paul loewen

community, bring together our understanding of the current situation and apply **logic** and reasoning, interpret **Scripture** as best we know how, appeal to the **Holy Spirit** through prayer, and then make a decision.

God will not abandon us because we make a wrong decision,[7] from His or our own perspective. God's will in this world is bigger than our little decisions, and doesn't rely on us doing something specific for it to come about. We, along with God, are working creatively[8] towards a beautiful future of re-creation and restoration.[9] What a beautiful opportunity: to be called, with freedom and opportunities, to work alongside with God as we become the kind of people God meant us to be.

As I close this chapter, I want to finish with a blog post from Donald Miller,[10] the author of "Blue Like Jazz." It beautifully sums up what I've said, and always leaves me with hope and excitement as I seek to understand what my life might hold. Enjoy :)

> I want to write an essay saying the statistical chance of God having a specific plan for your life is roughly 1 in 227. I'd base that statistic on Scripture, because Scripturally, for every one person God had a specific plan for, there were 226 He did not. Joseph was in, Benjamin was out, and so on.
>
> Okay, I haven't actually done the math. It may be 1 in 250 or 1 in 95, but that is hardly

---

[7] See chapter 1.

[8] See chapter 8.

[9] See chapter 3.

[10] http://storylineblog.com/2010/04/29/does-god-have-a-specific-plan-for-your-life-probably-not/

the point. The point is we think God is going to tell us exactly what to do, but chances are, He isn't. It's just not a Biblical idea.

God does have a general desire for everybody: for them to be reunited with the Trinity through Christ, and for them to have food and shelter and relationships, but I don't believe God has mapped out a plan for your every day, or even for your every year.

My friends who disagree and think God has a specific plan for everybody are mostly sitting around waiting to hear from God. Meanwhile, God's plan for them, apparently, is to shop at Bed Bath and Beyond and quote the latest Saturday Night Live skit. Quite the plan.

I contend with this idea for a number of reasons, but the main reason is that I don't think God is a control freak.

Imagine visiting a friend's house for dinner for the first time. You sit down at the table and the father, who sits at the head of the table, tells each of the kids, and the wife for that matter, what and when to eat. Then he tells them what to wear to bed, when they will be getting up, where they will be going to college and who they will be married to. Later, you tell your friend you thought their dad might be a bit controlling. You secretly believe their family to be dysfunctional. But your friend is offended. They think it's perfectly normal to want to please their father in everything they do. And they are right, it is appropriate to want to please one's father. The only problem is, their father is NUTS!

God, on the other hand, isn't nuts.

If God is fathering us, He is helping us discover what is good, right, pure, and worthy to pursue. He teaches us morality and ethics, but also gave us a heart filled with desire and longing. It's as though God sets before us a big sheet of butcher paper and hands us a box of crayons and tells us to dream.

I've a friend whose wife is a counselor who does this very experiment with kids she counsels. She gives them a sheet of paper and some crayons, and based on how they respond, she can tell whether or not the child has a dysfunctional relationship with their parents.

But I could be wrong. Here's how you know, based on Scripture, whether God has a specific plan for your life:

1. If you are a virgin and you get pregnant anyway.
2. If your donkey talks to you.
3. If an angel wants to wrestle.

If any of this happens to you, God is definitely at work. He also wants you to see a counselor.

And there are a few more. You get the point. If God has something specific for you, you'll know, I promise. But if He is setting a box of crayons down in front of you (a box of crayons called life) then by all means draw. He's taught you right from wrong, good from bad, beautiful from profane, so draw. He will be with you, proud of you, cheering you on, so draw. He loves you, so draw in the inspiration of the knowledge of His love. Draw a purple horse, a red ocean, a nine-legged dog, it doesn't matter. Let's stop being so afraid. Let's live, and show the world what it really means to be grateful we don't live in a dysfunctional family.

before
i go
8
jesus' third way

Picture this: you're playing an intense game of dodgeball when a guy gets hit hard - where it hurts. He's ticked off, and he's got a temper. He comes storming across the gym towards the thrower, fist pulled back and ready to fly. You've got less than a second to make a decision: what do you do?

Now this: you're walking across the school field with two friends when you see a group of six guys walking across your path. They're bigger than you, meaner than you, and, when they catch a glimpse of you guys, start heading your way. One of your friends has gotten on their bad side in the past, and they're starting to make fun of him. There are three of you, six of them. The odds don't look good, and the bullying is getting worse: what do you do?

Then this: your older sister is athletic, and you've always been competitive. You're on the backyard rink, skating and taking shots at her (she's in net, so it's okay). At some point, you miss the net and she decides it's a good moment to make fun of your aim. You're skating right towards her: what do you do?

And this: you're in grade 6, and you're a small kid. Smaller than almost everyone in your grade, and even smaller than kids a few years younger than you. Two boys - both in grade 5 - have taken to following you around at school and calling you names. No one else seems to notice, no one else seems to care. It's been happening for days and you've kept your cool, but it's getting worse and no one is looking: what do you do?

We'll take a pause from the stories at this point, and stop to ask the big question: how, as Christians, are we called to respond to the bad in this world? There are a few ways we might answer.

On the one hand, we might say we're called to seek justice and get rid of evil through whatever method is needed. Christians throughout history have gone this route and sometimes it's worked and sometimes it hasn't.

On the other hand, you might say it's our duty to extend God's love and mercy to everyone, never fighting back, regardless of what that might mean for our own personal safety. Christians throughout history have gone this route and sometimes it's worked and sometimes it hasn't.

Responses come in all shapes and sizes, including the entire spectrum between those two options.

Second big question: does our response to bad and evil change depending on if it's **big** or **small**, **global** or **personal**?

Maybe we can avoid conflict when it's personal, but global evil needs to be confronted. Maybe we can use nonviolence for small problems, but big conflicts demand a violent response. Is there a one-size-fits-all response to conflict?

Back to the stories.

The two name-calling bullies were coming toward me, and I let the adrenaline take control. They were of different sizes (one about my size, the other significantly bigger). I punched the big one in the stomach and, while he keeled over, grabbed the little one and threw him a few feet into the snow. No one saw me do it, and I never got in trouble. I walked away, and they never bothered me again.

I was skating towards my sister in net, and I used my stick to cross-check her backwards into the crossbar. The inevitable yelling and blaming followed, and I got in trouble. I wouldn't get good at controlling my temper for a few years still.

The six guys were coming towards us, and my friend they were ridiculing started to make comments back at them. It wasn't looking good. We were able to get him to keep quiet, but it wasn't improving the situation. Then, almost like a movie scene, at the back of the group I recognized one of the six. We had been in the cross-country running club together, and had spent many an afternoon running up and down Rothesay. He was the complete opposite of me, but we had good conversations. As he saw us, our eyes connected. Ten steps away from what would have been a one-sided bullying situation, he called it quits. "Let's drop it guys," he said, "I know them. They're cool." And they all walked away.

The kid who was about to clock the thrower was only a few steps away, and thankfully I was close. I took the only action I could think of: I stepped in front of the target and yelled, from three feet away, into the face of the would-be attacker, "Hit me!" For some reason, the combination of someone stupid enough to step in the way, to demand to be hit, and to not back down threw him off. I yelled again, "If you need to hit someone, hit me!" He backed down.

In all four cases, **the immediate problem was resolved**: the two grade 5 boys stopped bugging me, my sister took me seriously, the 6 guys backed off, and the dodgeballer stepped down. In two of the situations, I responded with violence. In two, I didn't.

Here's the reality: in the problems I resolved with violence, the bad **stopped** but nothing good **started**.

For the remainder of that school year, the two boys did not look at me or come near me. I ran into one of them a few years ago in the grocery store. He was behind me in the line by a few people. I **knew** he saw me, but he looked away. And he would not make eye contact with me. Roughly a dozen years later, our relationship was **still** broken. What happened between 11- and 12-year-olds separated 25-year-olds.

My sister stopped making fun of me, but our relationship remained strained while I had temper issues. It wasn't until years later, as a teenager, when we'd reconnect and become friends. By that point I had learned to not lash out with force.

And the beautiful outcome of the problems I solved non-violently was this: bad stopped **and** good started.

In the case of the 6 guys, they learned my name later and would nod at me in the hallway. I never had to worry about them bugging me (or that friend) again.

In the case of the potential dodgeball attack, the kid who had a temper issue saw me in a new way. We got to know each other better, our church gave their family a hamper at Christmas, and by the time our relationship parted ways (they moved away) he respected me as a person. He also, from that point forward, didn't fight other kids.

The reality is violence may solve the **short-term** problem, but often creates a **long-term** one. Nonviolence, on the other hand, seeks to get **underneath** the problem. Why do people hurt so much inside that they need to lash out at others? Why do our tempers flare, causing problems for others and ourselves? Every time we act out in violence, we simply pass it on to another person. Whoever we bully will probably bully another. Whoever is bullying is probably bullied by someone else.

The beauty about non-violence is it stops the domino effect at the start, it tells violence it has no power and will not continue, and it shortens the healing process.

As Mennonites, we are pacifists. This goes back to our beginnings some five hundred years ago, and it continues today. We remember the story of Dirk Willems, who was running across ice when his pursuer fell through. Dirk turned to rescue him, resulting in Dirk being captured and eventually martyred for his faith. Though you have grown up in the Mennonite church and are used to the idea of pacifism, it's actually only a small percentage of the global church that is pacifist. Even within pacifist churches, many people hold to partial pacifism, without fully jumping onboard.

Part of the problem, I believe, comes from our misunderstanding of the word. When we read the word **pacifism**, we often hear **passivism**. Being passive means doing nothing, more or less allowing ourselves to get stepped on. On the other hand, **pacifism** is simply the belief that violence is against what we believe. The word itself says nothing about being a doormat. Rather, pacifism is about working for peace. Peace, in the biblical sense, is more than the absence of war. It's based on **shalom**, a word which means equal parts wholeness, completeness, rest, comfort, and the absence of war.

In Matthew 5:38-42, Jesus says, "You have heard that it was said, 'Eye for eye, and tooth for tooth.' But I tell you, do not resist an evil person. If anyone slaps you on the right cheek, turn to them the other cheek also. And if anyone wants to sue you and take your shirt, hand over your coat as well. If anyone forces you to go one mile, go with them two miles. Give to the one who asks you, and do not turn away from the one who wants to borrow from you."

At first glance, this seems to promote **passivism**, like Jesus is telling us to do nothing in response to bullying, oppression, and systematic violence. In most settings, when discussing an issue of violence, people will often talk about the **fight** or **flight** instincts. Basically, our mind decides to take one of two responses: fight back physically, or run away as fast as we can. Jesus doesn't seem to argue for either of those two, but introduces a third way.[1] And just like many topics we've addressed in this book, it takes a better understanding of the culture around the story to get Jesus' point. The reality is Jesus' audience would probably have been shocked by what he said - not because he discouraged violence, but because he encouraged creative, overthrowing actions.

---

[1] All credit for this interpretation of Matthew 5:38-42 goes to Walter Wink.

Jesus uses three examples, and each is counter-cultural in its approach.

First, the slapping situation. Here, the victim is turning the other cheek. The details are important. The person is being slapped on the right cheek, not the left. Reach out your hand and pretend to slap someone. Which cheek did you (pretend to) hit? If you're right-handed, it would be their left cheek. If you're left-handed, well, you wouldn't have been allowed to be left-handed back then.[2]

So hitting on the right cheek was only possible with a **backhanded slap**.[3] This is the kind of slap reserved for putting someone in their place. In other words, it was the kind of slap the dominant person would use on the subservient, for men to use against women, parents against kids, masters against slaves.

The situation Jesus is describing here is one of **dominance** and **oppression**, where the person doing the slapping is clearly the authority. In most situations, the person being slapped would cower and "behave," following the instructions and authority of the slapper.

Jesus, however, tells the slapped to turn the **other cheek**. He's not saying to get hit again. He's saying to offer the left cheek. A left-cheek slap was a slap reserved for equals, for men against men. To reject the right-cheek slap and offer your left cheek was to say to the person: "I will not be abused. I will not be oppressed."

---

[2] Left-handedness has been seen as evil throughout history. My dad was left-handed but was taught to use his right. He can still play ping-pong well with both hands.

[3] The left hand was used, back then, for wiping after using the washroom. It wasn't used in normal interpersonal interactions.

paul loewen

What was a simple moment of someone degrading an inferior has become an embarrassing moment where they are challenged. Their options are limited: they can walk away in defeat or they can slap them as an equal. Anyone nearby would know the tables have turned, and the one who had the power no longer does.

Second, the cloak situation. For this one we go to the Old Testament. Deuteronomy 24 says, "If your neighbour is poor and gives you his cloak as security for a loan, do not keep the cloak overnight. Return the cloak to its owner by sunset so he can stay warm through the night and bless you, and the Lord your God will count you as righteous." The important word here is **poor**.

Essentially, the person is so poor they can only offer their outer cloak as collateral for a loan. Collateral is essentially what you give up if you can't afford to pay someone back. Let's say you're in a restaurant and you realize you've forgotten your wallet. You could let them hold your phone while you run home to get money. If you don't come back, they keep your phone. That's collateral.

In the story Jesus is telling, the person being sued is so poor all they can offer for collateral, and what the oppressor is demanding, is their shirt. Jesus tells the victim here to hand over their shirt and their cloak. Basically, give them **everything** you have. At first glance this looks like another situation of being walked on, but it's not.

If all you have to offer is your shirt, and you take it (and your jacket) and hand it to the person suing you, you're effectively saying, "This is it. This is all I have. Take it, since you've ruined my life." If you were wealthy and could pay them off easily, your money wouldn't raise any eyebrows in a court. But by stripping down, you've exposed yourself,[4] showing the true damage of their oppression and injustice. You've pinned them into an awkward spot, and reversed the position of power. They have been exposed as an oppressor, and you've shown the system to be corrupt.

Third, the walk-a-mile situation. At first glance, this also looks like it's about being used and exploited. Here, someone has demanded you walk a mile, and you've decided to continue walking and go two miles.

In Jesus' time, the only people who could force you to walk a mile were Roman soldiers. Rome controlled the region, and the constant presence of soldiers reminded all the Jews. When traveling, the soldiers could demand of local people to carry soldiers' packs. There was, however, a limit: they could force someone to carry the pack for a mile, but no farther.

Picture the situation now: the victim was walking along, the soldier came up from behind, threw out a few derogatory words, and handed over a heavy pack. Forced to stumble along for a mile, the victim would come to the end of their service. At that point the soldier would take the pack back, but that's not what Jesus is advocating. Instead, he says, **keep going**.

By going beyond the mile and walking for a second, the victim could cause trouble for the soldier from their superiors. In effect, the victim here has taken

---

4 Some argue this goes even further, because nudity was embarrassing in their society for the person viewing the nudity. In other words, being naked wasn't a disgrace but **seeing** nakedness was. If that's the case, then stripping completely down in the middle of court would force everyone present to look away and be ashamed. Again, even further flipping the power of the situation.

the power back in the situation. At the end of the mile, as the victim continued to walk with the pack, the soldier would be forced to beg for the pack back. Instead of being in authority, now they're forced to lower themself to avoid the trouble.

Again, as the victim you've exposed an oppressor and shamed injustice. Each of these actions have the same goal: overturning the power structure of the time.

It's not about lying down; it's about **standing up**.

Take away the oppressor's power without violence. Expose injustice without hurting anyone. Raise yourself, the oppressed, from your position of weakness.

What Jesus is advocating is cultural defiance.

It's possible violence would solve the immediate problem, but Jesus' approach aims at the underlying oppression and injustice. It raises the weak and lowers the powerful, something Jesus declared he was here to do in Luke 4 when he quotes Isaiah by saying, "He has sent me to proclaim freedom for the prisoners and recovery of sight for the blind, to set the oppressed free, to proclaim the year of the Lord's favour."[5] He takes those words on himself, saying, "Today this scripture is fulfilled in your hearing."

As a baby, Jesus had these words spoken over him, "This child is destined to cause the falling and rising of many in Israel,"[6] by Simeon. At Jesus' baptism,

---

[5] The Year of the Lord's Favour refers to the Jubilee. See chapter 5.

[6] Luke 2:34.

John said, "Every valley shall be filled in, every mountain and hill made low."[7]

This idea of leveling the playing field is woven into the very fabric of Jesus' life, right from birth.

If **flight** is the first option, and **fight** is the second, then this idea, of subverting the powerful systems and exposing injustice through **nonviolent action**,[8] is Jesus' third way.

If you're ever in a confrontational violent situation,[9] those three options present themselves.

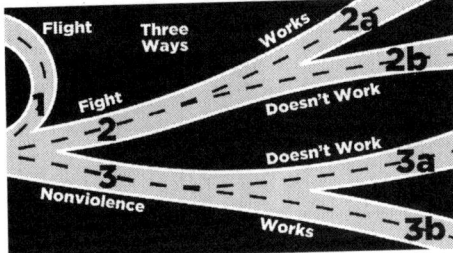

Option 1, flight: Turn and take off. Doesn't solve the immediate problem or the long-term problem.

Option 2, fight: If you've got fists, use them. If you've got a baseball bat, go for it. If you've got a gun, threaten and then, if they don't listen, aim. Within this option, there are two outcomes:

---

[7] Luke 3:5.

[8] When you talk about nonviolent actions, definitions become important. For instance, is holding a person back nonviolent or violent? If you understand violence as physical action intended to harm, then holding someone is nonviolent. The key word is also **intention**, as in, the goal behind your action. If you had to put actions on a spectrum and draw a line somewhere, my guess is it's somewhere between tackling and punching.

[9] Or even a hypothetical one, because the minute you tell someone you're a pacifist they're bound to say, "What if someone came into your house and threatened your family?"

paul loewen

Option 2a, fighting works: You've solved the immediate problem, but at the expense of hurting another human being. You've also now committed violence and, depending on the weapon you had in your hand, possibly seriously injured or killed someone. The long-term problem has probably escalated, since now they (if they're still alive) or their family/friends (if the victim is not still alive) will look for revenge.

Option 2b, fighting doesn't work: You did what you could, but couldn't take them down. The situation is worse now, since

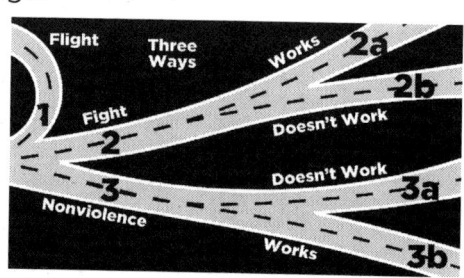

they're angered and motivated. Given that they were already prone to violence, they're less likely to stop than they were before. So you've put yourself or your family into a situation that has escalated. At the same time, you have committed violence and will have to deal with the guilt later. That is, if you survive.

Option 3, nonviolent action: You try to surprise your attacker with words, strange actions, compassion, or mercy. You turn the tables and hope for the best.

Option 3a, nonviolent action doesn't work: It's possible it won't work, and your situation won't improve. Perhaps they'll still go through with their original violent act. However, you won't have escalated the situation, you haven't hurt anyone, you've stayed true to what you believe, and you have, especially if your story is told, inspired others. Throughout history many pacifists have looked to martyrs (people who died for their faith) as their inspiration.

Option 3b, nonviolent action works: Way to go!
You restrain, surprise, confound, or discombobulate
the person. You've solved the immediate danger
and perhaps exposed what was underneath the
violent action. You have respected the individual,
and de-escalated this and future situations.

In John Howard Yoder's book "What Would You
Do?" he walks through these (and a few more)
options for outcomes,[10] then gives awesome
examples where these strategies work. For instance,
there's a woman who woke up with a stranger in her
bedroom. She asked him what the time was, he -
completely surprised - answered, and they
conversed. She asked him to sleep on the couch
downstairs and they'd talk in the morning. He left
the next day without hurting anyone. Or, the elderly
lady who was being followed by two young men
while walking with her groceries. Rather than get
robbed, she turned around and asked if they would
carry her groceries for her. Surprised, they
answered yes and walked her home. My dodgeball
story from the beginning of this chapter is another
example of surprise turning the situation around.

The real question, when looking at the options: what
is the preferred outcome? I have no doubt most
people would agree option 3b, nonviolent action
working, is the best outcome. There's no doubt
option 2b, violent action not working, is the worst
outcome. When people make the decision to fight,
they're not picturing 2b. They're picturing,
somehow, they will kung-fu themselves out of a
situation or be able to aim steady in the most
intense moment of their lives. They're picturing 2a.
The real question is whether they consider the

---

[10] He also adds the option for a miracle to happen. By
moving to violence, we are effectively shutting the door
to God's intervention.

possible failure of nonviolent action better or worse than the possible success of fighting.

For a pacifist, 3a is always better than 2a **or** 2b. The long-term good of remaining true to what they believe, respecting the other individual, and exposing injustice far outweighs the short-term good of violent action, and especially outweighs the short-term (and long-term) bad of committing violence oneself.

Moving down the path of violence means closing yourself off from nonviolence. Once you have made that decision, there is no going back. You have now limited yourself to a 50/50 chance of violence working or not working (for a person like me, who has never been in a real fight or fired a gun, the odds of it working are much less than 50/50). The risks of it not working, and even the negative aspects of it working, for me, are not worth going down that path.

Nonviolent action holds a better chance of long-term change in the attacker's life and even, I believe, the resolution of the short-term problem. This is why, as much as I can control my body's instincts, I aim to subvert and overturn violent actions with nonviolent responses. It gives me the best odds of success and the lowest odds of ending up the victim.

There are inevitably fears and questions: what if I die? What about war?

To the first I say: Jesus doesn't promise it will work. In many cases, Jesus actually claims it will lead to hardship and possibly pain or persecution. But the fact it might not work does not erase its value. If it doesn't solve the short-term problem, it's possible it will have an impact in the long term. When people die for their beliefs, others are inspired. Take, for instance, the forgiveness offered by an Amish community that had a killer take away the lives of some of their children.[11] They have become an example, for millions of people, of what grace and forgiveness can look like.

To the second I say: nonviolence has been successful in curbing and even stopping significant violent movements in the past.[12] Gandhi's actions in the Indian independence movement is one of the best examples. Even in WWII, there were small isolated groups that used nonviolent techniques against the Nazis. In WWI, the Christmas spirit led troops in opposing bunkers to cease fighting[13] - a game of soccer even broke out between the Germans and the British.[14] In order to get them to fight again, their superiors had to move them to other combat zones because they didn't want to fight their newfound friends. In the 60s, the American Civil Rights movement was successful largely **because** of nonviolent action undertaken by Martin Luther King Jr. and others.

At the same time, it is critically important for me to admit we benefit from a military protecting our borders. It is far easier to speak eloquently on this subject in our relatively safe world. I can never promise I will hold 100% fast to my commitment in times of violence, war, or terrorism. However, I **can** point to the people who, in the face of personal and

---

[11] https://en.wikipedia.org/wiki/West_Nickel_Mines_School_shooting

[12] These examples, and others, are from http://www.dailygood.org/story/784/30-examples-of-successful-non-violent-action-bk-community/

[13] One of the coolest stories. Check it out at https://en.wikipedia.org/wiki/Christmas_truce

[14] It is believed the Germans won 3-2.

global violence, have stood their ground and held their beliefs. I point you in their direction, not mine.

But even pointing to those people isn't enough. And so I finally point to Jesus. He spoke the words, painted the vision, and followed it to his death. Jesus' path was one of nonviolence to the end. He commanded his disciples not to fight back, he led himself "like a lamb to the slaughter"[15] to be crucified for us, and his sacrificial nonviolent death was the ultimate victory over death itself.

So when you think nonviolence can't work, look to the cross.

Look to Jesus.

---

[15] Isaiah 53:7.

before
i go

your identity is in christ

When it comes to how we measure, not all systems are created equal.[1]

The inch was originally the width of a man's thumb.[2] Given the variance in the size of people, I imagine that was difficult to keep track of. King Edward II finally ruled it would be equal to 3 grains of barley placed end-to-end lengthwise. Good luck next time you need to measure an inch.

The hand was approximately 5 inches or 5 digits (fingers) across. Today, it's been standardized to 4 inches and is used to measure horses (usually to the horse's shoulder).

---

[1] If you want to take a deep dive into why the imperial system doesn't make sense, watch the video here: https://www.youtube.com/watch?v=r7x-RGfd0Yk

[2] All of these come from http://www.factmonster.com/ipka/A0769529.html

paul loewen

A span is the length of a hand, stretched out. It's about 9 inches.

A yard was originally the length of a man's belt. Since, well, we know how different that can be from person to person, it probably was difficult to maintain. Finally King Henry I decided it would be the distance from his nose to the thumb of his outstretched arm. It's a little egotistical, in my mind, to make a measurement based on your own body, but to each his own! At some point it became defined as 36 inches (if your outstretched arm is that long you should be in the NBA).

The cubit (used frequently in the Bible) was the distance from the elbow to fingertips. Who decided all these would be based on body parts, which vary like crazy, is beyond me. I suppose at least they're always available.

The lick was used by the Greeks and was the distance from the tip of your thumb to index finger, or, in other terms, the scope of your finger gun you make at your friends when they're looking sharp.

The pace was used for defining marches. Originally a double step,[3] they were roughly 5 feet and when you took 1,000 paces you knew you had completed a mile (5,280 feet). Today, we count one step as a pace. For me, that's roughly 2.57 feet.[4]

Some of these make sense, and others are ridiculous. Now, we measure items in a more concrete way. For instance, a meter is defined by

---

[3] Not to be confused with dub step.

[4] I had to go and re-measure this to confirm, but the nerdiness in me already knew the number from years ago when I measured it out for fun. It's surprisingly helpful when you want to know approximate distances you can walk quickly. Just pace it out and multiply.

how far light travels in a vacuum[5] in 1/299,792,458th of a second.[6] Usain Bolt, for comparison, covers a metre in 1/13th of a second.[7] So, light is approximately 22 million times faster than Usain. Measuring based on something that doesn't change (like the speed of light) makes more sense than measuring based on each person's waist or the King's arm.

When it comes to measuring, having something external and concrete to measure by makes the most sense.[8] Measuring anything by a **changing** standard is a terrible idea.

Take a minute to finish this next sentence, and feel free to do it multiple times with whatever comes to mind:

I am a _____.
I am a _____.
I am a _____.
I am a _____.

If you're like me, there are a few go-to answers. Here were mine: husband, father, pastor, student, friend, son, brother, writer, runner, dreamer. I could go on for a while. But they'd continue in that trend. All of these are based on something **outside** of ourselves, like how we measure ourselves.

---

[5] A vacuum, in this case, is something that has no air. If you would suck air out of a container with your household vacuum you'd create a vacuum.

[6] Light is ridiculously fast, if you didn't know.

[7] Based on a top speed of 30 miles per hour. His average speed when he ran the 9.58 world record was 23.5 miles per hour.

[8] This is demonstrated perfectly by the kilogram. There is a physical object defined as the kilogram held in a vacuum and never touched.

paul loewen

So, what are some ways people define or measure themselves?

When I have done this with you, we come up with about 30-40. For the sake of simplicity, we'll keep it to a nice dozen. Here are some of them:

Money
Education
Relationships
Looks
Athleticism
Accomplishments
Possessions
Virtues
Friends
Authority
Fame
Social Media

We'll put those aside for a minute, and look at a story from 2 Corinthians 11.

The Apostle Paul had an interesting history with the church in Corinth. In 1 Corinthians we realize the members of the church were debating on which Apostle they followed: Paul or Apollos. Apollos was an impressive speaker, and could convince people with persuasive words. Paul, on the other hand, seemed to stumble over his words when he was with them in person. But he was bold in his letters, demanding a lot from them. Apollos, too, had the credentials to prove that he deserved to be taken seriously. Paul didn't. So when we get to this part of 2 Corinthians, Paul was forced to defend his right to speak so strongly, to demand the church listen to what he had to say.

Even though he didn't want to, he decided it was time to engage in the game they're playing: listing his qualifications. "Am I a Hebrew?" he asked.

"Israelite? Servant of Christ?" He said, "I have done more and been more for Jesus: been in prison, been flogged, five times been whipped by the Jews, three times beaten with rods, once stoned, and three times shipwrecked."[9] If we're keeping track of who deserved to be listened to by the number of times the Jews had targeted him and how many times he'd been close to death and miraculously survived, Paul topped the list.

Paul makes a loud point here: "I don't want to define myself by the things you want, but I will. I don't want to measure according to the world's standards, but I will if you want." In the past he brought up various experiences: the vision he had of Jesus, the Holy Spirit coming on those he preached to, and, finally, simply being a brother with them through Jesus. Those are the things he'd rather be measured by, but the church forced him to play the silly games people play.

He'd rather appeal to Christ, through whom and by whom his life was dramatically changed.

But instead, he sounds as petty and foolish as the rest of us. He's been forced to use the standard measurements, since it's what the people have demanded of him.

And, by all practical standards, they **do** make sense. It's not ridiculous for a church to want to know their pastor has the right education, training, and worldview. If a church today didn't properly research the person they were hiring, they'd be seen as foolish. So while we look at what Paul just had to say as foolish, we also deeply resonate with him. It doesn't seem strange today, in a world where we can do a background check on people by looking them up on Facebook. What the church was

---

9 Paraphrased by me.

asking was more or less the modern equivalent of checking Paul's references. Frustrated that they don't seem to understand that the message of Jesus isn't about credentials, he's forced to put his credentials, as foolish as it might seem, on display.

Think back to the twelve measuring sticks we listed: money, education, relationships, looks, athleticism, accomplishments, possessions, virtues, friends, authority, fame, and social media. These make sense on the surface. **Money** is one of the most common standards, so why shouldn't it also apply to us? **Education** generally means someone has worked hard and may know more, so it's not completely invalid. The number of **friends** someone has may speak volumes about their character, compassion, and ability to have fun. We could do this with all 12 standards, and we'd find positive aspects for all of them. Often they show hard work, determination, and maybe a little luck.

On the other hand, there are some serious weaknesses in using money as our standard. Whether we have a lot of money or a higher education is partially dependent on our effort, yes, but also on where we were born and what our parents did for work. I, for instance, am more likely to have a comfortable middle-class life than someone born in a developing country as one child among ten. Every day I heard my dad wake up at 6 a.m. to go to work, and that example is forever forged in my memory, reminding me what it looks like to work. Not everyone is fortunate enough to have that demonstrated to them.

It's time to judge those twelve standards, and see if they pass our test.

We'll judge them by two criteria:
  1. Are they temporary or long-lasting?

2. Are they dependent on our effort or out of our control?

I'll list them, then let you circle the number that makes the most sense in each category. Use a different colour for each (ex. Use black for temporary vs long-lasting, and red for out of our control vs our effort).

Colour 1:	Temporary			Long-Lasting	
Colour 2:	Out of our Control			Our Effort	
Money	1	2	3	4	5
Education	1	2	3	4	5
Relationships	1	2	3	4	5
Looks	1	2	3	4	5
Athleticism	1	2	3	4	5
Accomplish-ments	1	2	3	4	5
Possessions	1	2	3	4	5
Virtues	1	2	3	4	5
Friends	1	2	3	4	5
Authority	1	2	3	4	5
Fame	1	2	3	4	5
Social Media	1	2	3	4	5

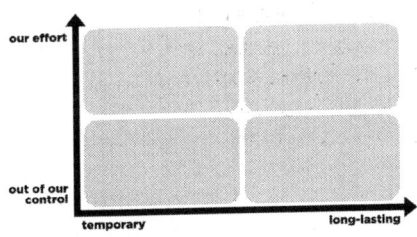

For each one, you might have a radically different perspective than I do. That's fine, and you'll see why in a bit. I've made a graph for you to plot your answers, and see where they fall. On the bottom is temporary vs long-lasting and on the side is out of our control vs our effort (go back and look at what you chose for each). It might take some time, but plot your answers and see where they fall. I've also shown my answers on a graph. I could get into why I put them where I put them, but it's not necessary.

paul loewen

The bottom-left corner is the one to stay away from. It's the corner where temporary meets out of our control. In other words, if we base

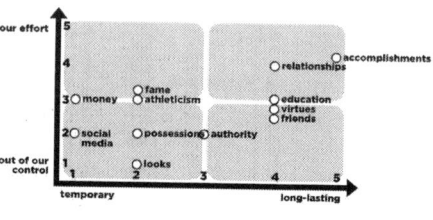

our identity on these factors we'll be terribly unhappy with how we are doing. Not only do they not last long, but we may not even have had anything to do with us receiving them. In this corner I put looks, social media, and possessions. It's no wonder that in our current culture, where we put so much value on these temporary and out-of-our-own-control things, people have enormous self-esteem issues.

Next up for discussion is the top-left corner, where temporary meets things that are dependent on our effort. In other words, we can work really hard to earn these things, and we may achieve them. We might even experience happiness, but we'll soon discover that it doesn't last. It's no wonder that people who have climbed these ladders look down and say, "It's not as great as I thought it would be." Tim Cook, the CEO of the biggest company in the world (Apple), said, "Don't work for money - it will wear out fast, or you'll never make enough and you will never be happy."[10] Into this category I put money, fame, and athleticism. If these qualities were great ways to define ourselves, we'd expect richer countries and/or richer people to experience lower levels of depression. Spoiler: they don't.[11]

---

[10] http://www.cnbc.com/2017/02/09/apple-ceo-tim-cook-dont-work-for-money-you-will-never-be-happy.html

[11] http://www.livescience.com/35792-global-depression-rates.html

Cross to the other corner of the chart, and we have the area where long-lasting meets out-of-our-control. In other words, these are stabilizing, helpful standards in our lives that can provide satisfaction and happiness. However, it's most likely a luck-of-the-draw situation as to how well we end up doing. As I said earlier, where we are born, the circles we grow up in, and the experiences that we have - these are based on external forces that we can't control. Into this category I put authority, virtues, and friends. If these factors define us, we may find ourselves suddenly having the rug pulled out from under our feet.

Finally, the top-right corner is the one to aim for: the intersection of long-lasting and our effort. If we're going to base our identity on anything, it would seem logical that we'd want to base it on these. Here, we'll find that if we work hard enough to do well in these categories we can establish long-lasting satisfaction and happiness. Here I put education, relationships, and accomplishments. Even as I say those, I am well aware that you could counter-argue each point. But, in particular, education and accomplishments are past experiences that cannot be taken away from you. Relationships, particularly family ones, are eternal (even if they're broken). The quality of each of these is what is up to our effort. With these in our hands, we can ride out the ups-and-downs of life.

For the most part.

Let's go back to the story of Paul from 2 Corinthians 11, because it didn't end there. He had just listed (to his own annoyance) what the Corinthian church wanted from him: his qualifications, experience, and authority. "If you need me to, I'll do it," he said. He doesn't stop there, however.

"If I'm going to keep this boasting going,"[12] he said, "I'm going to boast in the things that make me weak. One time I barely escaped with my life with the King out to kill me. Oh, and I'll boast about my friend who's had all these visions!" (He's most likely talking about himself here, again caving to what they want to hear.) "Rather, I'll boast about the things that make me weak. Because in my weakness, God is made strong. In my weakness, God shows His power. When I fail, God's power works through me. That's why I'm willing to talk about all the times I've nearly died - not because they prove something about my authority, but because **when I am weak, then I am strong**."

By all practical standards, Paul had decent credentials. And he was willing to roll them out, but it's not what he wants to focus on. Instead, he'll list his weaknesses to prove a point: it's God that makes him strong.

Paul took our grid of standards and obliterated them - even the top-right corner. All of these, he says, are useless. Even the most long-lasting and best (in our perspective) standards **will not last**. Education can become meaningless as we age, accomplishments no longer provide the satisfaction they once did, and relationships can struggle and falter like we do as people. Not even the best of our standards can live up to the test of time, or stand strong through our own effort.

If we base our value on anything short of God we will never measure up, our value will never last, and we will never be satisfied with what we have achieved, earned, or received.

Perhaps you're like me, and the default standard upon which you base your value is

---

[12] All of these are paraphrased.

accomplishments and money.[13] No amount of money will ever be enough, and accomplishments are addicting but fade with time. It will not last.

Maybe you base your value on the number of good friends you have, and the people who invite you over. One day you'll find yourself getting rejected, wishing you had different friends or needing just one more. Your value will not last.

Or maybe you base your value on your volunteer record, your physical attractiveness, your social media following, your career, your authority, or your PhD. You won't be fifteen or twenty years old forever, a thousand retweets won't hold the buzz it used to, you'll eventually be replaced at work by the younger generation, someone else will come along who can whip the crowd into a frenzy, and eventually the letters behind your name will just be a long string that people struggle to pronounce. It will not last.

It will not last.

There is **nothing** that we can base our identity on within the realm of what we currently know that will last for even our lifetime, nevermind beyond our lives. Those who base their identity on their work will, one day, as the next generation takes their place, find themselves suddenly without a purpose (cue the mid-life crisis). Those who base their identity on relationships may, one day, find they are the next subject of the gossip.

Rather, we need to base our identity on something outside of ourselves, outside of our current understanding. That is Christ.

---

13 I'm working on it, I really am. This chapter could easily be a letter I wrote myself.

paul loewen

Right, you say. And what does that **mean**?

Let's go back to the "I am" statements. Every one I made (and, most likely, that you made as well) was defined over and against something. There was always a word that followed the "I am," whatever it was. It may have been something trivial (like in the bottom-left corner) or something significant (in the upper-right corner). Either way, there was something we had to measure ourselves against, a standard which we had so others would understand either who we are or what our worth is. Depending on a standard also introduces competition, because we don't just want to be defined against that standard but also in **comparison** to the next person, making sure we have more than they do.

Interestingly, the name that we have for God from the Old Testament is Yahweh.[14] When Moses meets God, God uses the name Yahweh. We understand Yahweh to mean, "I am who I am." In other words, God doesn't need a standard to measure who God is. Simply put, "I am" is enough. God is. Where we scramble for words and standards by which to define ourselves, God simply is. Outside of our understanding of time, space, and experience, God is.

Since our standards fail, we should hitch our wagon to God - a powerful undefinable. Where all of our current standards fail, God exists outside of all of them. It is only when we define ourselves by a standard that is undefinable, by something that is

---

[14] Actually, the name we have is YHWH. There were no vowels in the Hebrew. We've filled in the gaps with what we think is the most logical, and came up with Yahweh. When YHWH is used in the Old Testament our English translations usually say, The LORD. YHWH was the name of God that the Jews refused to say out loud (because of how special it was), and they often referred to Him as "Elohim," which would translate simply as God.

concrete, permanent, beyond anything else, that we can move forward with confidence in our identity.

To do this requires replacing our stories about who we are. It requires changing the end of our "I am" statements from temporary standards and definitions to, "a child of God." As we saw in chapter 1 (God Loves You), the love of God is not something that can be taken from us.

Within ourselves, we carry stories that pull us away from God. Perhaps they are reminders of how we have failed, how we aren't as good as those around us, how we have done things that are unforgivable. Whether we realize it or not, we act out of these stories every day.

God, the "I Am," is not a God that marks or evaluates us the same way the world does. Jesus reminds us, story after story, that God loves sinners, regardless of performance or faithfulness. These stories need to replace our internal stories.

It's the difference of changing "I'm a terrible person" to "I'm being redeemed by God." Or, "I will never make a difference" to "I can show love to those around me." Or, "I can get through life on my own" to "God's forgiveness extends to even me."

When it comes down to it, we are much harsher judges of our character than God is. Because of Jesus, when God looks at us He doesn't judge us with the same criticisms we use on ourselves. Rather, He sees us through the lens of Jesus' death, through the hope He offers to everyone on the planet.

Replacing the stories we tell about ourselves with God's story for us means we need to grab onto the truths we know about God's perspective. To close, I'll leave you with three that have been important to me. May their claims take root in your heart, replacing the stories you've been telling yourself, grow into an identity that isn't held captive by the standards of the world, and flower into a future based in who God is.

Acts 17:28, "For in him we live and move and have our being."

John 15:5, Jesus talking, "I am the vine; you are the branches. If you remain in me and I in you, you will bear much fruit; apart from me you can do nothing."

1 John 3:1, "See what great love the Father has lavished on us, that we should be called children of God! And that is what we are!"[15]

---

[15] A great song to put on your playlist to cement these stories in your memory is "Good, Good Father" by Chris Tomlin!

thank you

Thank you to my lovely wife Jeanette, for working with me for the first years of our ministry, for encouraging me to take the time to write this book, and for being my first and most important sounding board in all the work I do.

Thank you to Carl DeGurse, for taking on the task of editing this book for me. It was fascinating to see the mistakes I was blind to, and to see how much better it could be by removing about 75% of my uses of the words "that" and "thing" from each chapter.

Thank you to the Douglas youth, for whom this book was written. I have seen many of you come and go over my ten years here. Every time a grade graduates, I am amazed I can love and appreciate the new grade just as much! This book was for you, partially by you (without your knowledge), and I hope it inspires and reminds you of God's goodness.

paul loewen

Thank you to the youth leaders, who have laughed with me and dreamt with me. Without you, none of this would have been possible, and you have been an incredible team to work with.

Thank you to the Douglas staff, who supported me through both good times and challenging times. Over the last ten years, I have always known that you would be there for me. I will miss our time in the office together.

Thank you to the Douglas community, for empowering and enabling me in the ministry here. It has been an honour to serve here, and I will look back on it fondly. I hope you can gain from this book as well.

Sincerely,

Paul Loewen
pauldloewen@gmail.com

Made in the USA
Middletown, DE
17 August 2017